FSOT
Practice Questions

FSOT Practice Test & Exam Review for the
Foreign Service Officer Test

Dear Future Exam Success Story:

First of all, **THANK YOU** for purchasing Mometrix study materials!

Second, congratulations! You are one of the few determined test-takers who are committed to doing whatever it takes to excel on your exam. **You have come to the right place.** We developed these practice tests with one goal in mind: to deliver you the best possible approximation of the questions you will see on test day.

Standardized testing is one of the biggest obstacles on your road to success, which only increases the importance of doing well in the high-pressure, high-stakes environment of test day. Your results on this test could have a significant impact on your future, and these practice tests will give you the repetitions you need to build your familiarity and confidence with the test content and format to help you achieve your full potential on test day.

Your success is our success

We would love to hear from you! If you would like to share the story of your exam success or if you have any questions or comments in regard to our products, please contact us at **800-673-8175** or **support@mometrix.com**.

Thanks again for your business and we wish you continued success!

Sincerely,
The Mometrix Test Preparation Team

TABLE OF CONTENTS

Practice Test #1

Job Knowledge

1. The current definition of the term "Latin America" is most correctly described as:

    a. Everywhere in the Americas that Spanish or Portuguese predominantly is spoken
    b. Everywhere in the Americas south of the United States, including the Caribbean
    c. Everywhere in the Americas where a Latinate (i.e. Romance) language is spoken
    d. All of the previous choices can correctly describe a current definition of the term "Latin America"

2. Which of the following is not considered a development of the Early Modern Period in history?

    a. Scientific experiments
    b. The early nation-states
    c. Progress in technology
    d. All of the above occurred during this period

3. The legislative structure set forth in the U.S. Constitution was determined by:

    a. The Virginia Plan
    b. The New Jersey Plan
    c. The Connecticut Compromise
    d. The Plan of Charles Pinckney

4. Which of the following is not true about the United States Constitution?

    a. It is the oldest written constitution still used by any country today
    b. Its first thirteen amendments make up the Bill of Rights document
    c. It is the shortest written constitution still used by any nation today
    d. It replaced the Articles of Confederation after a period of six years

5. Which of the following statements is correct regarding U. S. political parties?

    a. Democrat and Republican have been the two main parties since 1787
    b. The Democratic Party was first established in 1854
    c. The Republican Party was first established in 1824
    d. None of these statements is correct regarding U. S. political parties

6. Of the following, which characteristic does not embody a principle of Jeffersonian Democracy?

    a. Representation as a central value
    b. The separation of church and state
    c. Individual rights and states' rights
    d. Having a standing army and navy

7. Which Supreme Court ruling was the first to strike down a state law as unconstitutional?

    a. Fletcher v. Peck
    b. Marbury v. Madison
    c. Martin v. Hunter's Lessee
    d. McCullough v. Maryland

1

8. In 20th-century America, which of the following occurred first?

    a. The Emergency Quota Act was passed by Congress
    b. European immigration peaked at almost 1.3 million
    c. Congress passed a very restrictive Immigration Act
    d. The Great Depression caused decreased immigration

9. Who among the following people contributing to the Harlem Renaissance was actually African-American?

    a. Ridgely Torrence
    b. Carl van Vechten
    c. Claude McKay
    d. George Gershwin

10. Which of these U.S. Supreme Court decisions did not involve discrimination based on race?

    a. Korematsu v. United States (1944)
    b. Loving v. Virginia (1967)
    c. Jones v. Alfred H. Mayer Co. (1968)
    d. Frontiero v. Richardson (1973)

11. Which of the following firsts in space exploration did the U.S. accomplish?

    a. The first suborbital launch of a man-made rocket into outer space
    b. The first orbital launch of an unmanned satellite into outer space
    c. The first photos from space and first suborbital launch of animals
    d. The first launch of an orbital spacecraft with an animal on board

12. _____ was President of the United States when the Vietnam War began and _____ was President of the United States when it ended.

    a. Kennedy; Nixon
    b. Hoover; Kennedy
    c. Eisenhower; Ford
    d. Eisenhower; Nixon

13. Which of the following did not occur during the administration of President Bill Clinton?

    a. Clinton's terms of office saw a long period of economic expansion
    b. Hillary R. Clinton passed the Children's Health Insurance Program
    c. The Clintons tried to pass universal healthcare but were obstructed
    d. The House and Senate impeached Clinton for lying about an affair

14. Which of the following statements about immigration to the United States from 2000-2005 is incorrect?

    a. Less immigration to the United States occurred in these years than in other years
    b. More immigration to the United States occurred in these years than in other years
    c. There was greater border security in the United States after the 9/11 attacks
    d. Almost eight million persons immigrated to the U.S. at this time

15. Which of the following amendments is included in the Bill of Rights?

    a. The amendment stating states could not be sued by individuals
    b. The amendment stating that slavery was abolished in America
    c. The amendment stating that senators were to be elected directly
    d. The amendment stating non-federal powers were kept by states

16. Which of the following is a power held only by the federal government?

    a. The power to levy taxes, borrow money, and spend money
    b. The power to award copyrights and patents to people or groups
    c. The power to establish the criteria that qualify a person to vote
    d. The power to ratify proposed amendments to the Constitution

17. Of the following actions, which one requires a three-fourths majority?

    a. State approval of a proposed amendment to the Constitution
    b. Submitting a proposal for an amendment to the Constitution
    c. Ratification for appointments to the Presidency in the Senate
    d. The introduction of charges for an impeachment in the House

18. Which of the following is *not* correct about the growth of America in the first half of the 19th century?

    a. By 1840, two thirds of all Americans resided west of the Allegheny Mountains.
    b. The population of America doubled every 25 years during this time period.
    c. The trend of westward expansion increased as more people migrated west.
    d. Immigration to America from other countries was not substantial prior to 1820.

19. Of the following events, which one took place last?

    a. USSR launched the satellite Sputnik
    b. China produced an atomic bomb
    c. Soviet detonation of a hydrogen bomb
    d. US detonation of a hydrogen bomb

20. Which of the following was least associated with actions President Ronald Reagan took against Communism in his administration?

    a. His reinforcement of America's military weaponry
    b. His Strategic Defense Initiative for space defenses
    c. His Reagan Doctrine supporting freedom fighters
    d. His withdrawal of Cuban troops from Angola

21. Which of the following was not a part of President George H.W. Bush's "New World Order," initiated between 1989-1992 and following the end of the Cold War?

    a. The START I and START II treaties signed by the US and Russia
    b. Government reform in Nicaragua and the end of civil war in El Salvador
    c. The signing of NAFTA by three countries and its ratification by the Senate
    d. All of these were actions taken by the Bush administration from 1989-1992.

22. Of the following, which person or group was *not* instrumental in postwar advancement of civil rights and desegregation?
    a. The President
    b. The Supreme Court
    c. The Congress
    d. The NAACP

23. Of the following factors, which is not true regarding the US presidential election of 1992?
    a. George Bush's handling of the Persian Gulf War earned him high approval ratings.
    b. Bill Clinton received 47% of the votes while George Bush received 35% of votes.
    c. Problems with America's domestic economy worked against Bush in the election.
    d. Bill Clinton's campaign platform as a less liberal Democrat helped him in *the race.*

24. Which of the following is not true of issues in America during the Clinton administration?
    a. Due to objections, Clinton amended his suspension of the ban on gays in the military to a "don't ask-don't tell" policy.
    b. The Family and Medical Leave Act was passed in 1993, reforming employee policies in the event of family emergencies.
    c. President Clinton proposed the provision of universal health care coverage, but it was rejected by Congress.
    d. Clinton's plan to remedy the federal deficit via raising taxes and reducing federal spending was passed by Congress.

25. Which of the following statements regarding laws passed during the Clinton administration to control crime is not correct?
    a. The Brady Handgun Violence Prevention Act stipulated a five-day waiting period to buy a handgun.
    b. Following the shooting and consequent disability of James Brady, the "Brady Bill" passed without opposition.
    c. The Brady Handgun Violence Prevention Act allocated funds for a background-checking computer system.
    d. In 1994, Congress passed Clinton's bill to fund 100 000 additional police officer hires with over $8 billion.

26. Which of the following was not instrumental in enabling Republicans to take control of the House and the Senate in the 1994 Congressional elections during the Clinton administration?
    a. Alleged impropriety in the "Whitewater" deal
    b. Rumors alleging sexual misconduct by Clinton
    c. Debates on healthcare and gays in the military
    d. All of the above were factors that helped the Republicans gain control of Congress.

27. Which of the following statements regarding the 1998 impeachment of President Clinton is not correct?
    a. The grounds for impeachment were perjury and obstruction of justice.
    b. The House of Representatives voted for the impeachment of Clinton.
    c. The Senate voted to impeach before Clinton was acquitted of charges.
    d. Clinton first denied a relationship with Lewinsky, and then admitted to it.

28. Which of the following is not true about the use of computers in America?

    a. Mainframe computers existed in America beginning in 1946.
    b. The invention of microprocessors in the 1970s enabled the creation of a PC.
    c. The PC allowed the widespread use of computers by private citizens.
    d. PCs allowed the home use, but had less impact on businesses.

29. Of the following, which statement about the US economy in the 1990s is correct?

    a. By the year 2000, the US economy was increasing at a rate of 5% a year.
    b. The rate of unemployment in America at this time dropped to 6%.
    c. The rates of productivity and of inflation in the US were about the same.
    d. The US stock market's total value had doubled in only six years.

30. Which of the following statements regarding the Branch Davidians in 1993 is not true?

    a. The Branch Davidians were a Seventh Day Adventist sect living on a compound located near Waco, Texas.
    b. The Bureau of Alcohol, Tobacco, and Firearms got a search warrant for the Branch Davidian compound.
    c. When attempts to look for weapon stockpiles led to gunfire and deaths, the FBI attacked the compound.
    d. The incident at the Branch Davidian compound in Waco developed into a siege that lasted for two weeks.

31. Which statement regarding US international trade policy in the 1990s is incorrect?

    a. In 1994, the General Agreement on Tariffs and Trade (GATT) was approved by Congress.
    b. The GATT included 57 countries who agreed they would remove or reduce many of their tariffs.
    c. The GATT created the World Trade Organization (WTO) to settle international trade differences.
    d. The NAFTA (North American Free Trade Agreement), ratified in 1994, had originally been set up by George H.W. Bush's administration.

32. Which of the following statements about the presidential election of 2000 is not true?

    a. In this election, Democratic candidate Al Gore won the majority of the popular votes.
    b. Votes for Green Party candidate Ralph Nader diverted some votes from Gore.
    c. The state of Florida's electoral votes determined who won.
    d. When Gore demanded another recount in Florida, it yielded the exact same results.

33. Which of the following statements is not true regarding the events of September 11, 2001, in the US?

    a. Shortly after that date the US defeated the Taliban and captured Al-Qaeda leader Osama bin Laden.
    b. On September 11, 2001, Muslim terrorists flew two hijacked airplanes into the World Trade Center in New York.
    c. On September 11, 2001, Muslim terrorists flew a hijacked passenger airliner into the Pentagon in Arlington, Virginia.
    d. An airplane hijacked by Muslim terrorists crashed in Pennsylvania after passengers resisted the terrorists.

34. Which statement best describes the feudal society of Western Europe in the Middle Ages?

a. Religious institutions owned most of the land and leased portions to vassals.
b. Rulers granted land strictly on the basis of blood relationships.
c. Rulers granted vassals land in exchange for military and political service.
d. Feudalism shifted a spice-based economy to a land-based economy.

35. Which statement best describes the role of the Catholic Church in medieval Western Europe?

a. Powerful and wealthy, the Church was important to both poor and rich people.
b. The Church concerned itself mainly with the poorer members of medieval society.
c. Weakened by infighting about Church doctrine, the Church struggled to wield power.
d. The Catholic Church served as a neutral force between competing political leaders.

36. What effect did the Crusades have on Europe's Jewish population?

a. Entire European Jewish communities were killed during the First Crusade.
b. Persecution of Jewish people declined as the Crusaders focused on Muslims.
c. Most Jewish traders and merchants profited through Crusades-related business.
d. To avoid persecution, some Jewish-only battalions fought in each Crusade.

37. During the 15th century, Johann Gutenberg invented a printing press with moveable type. How did his invention influence science?

a. It did not influence science; the printing of Gutenberg Bibles directed public attention away from science and toward reforming the Catholic Church.
b. It led to scientific advances throughout Europe by spreading scientific knowledge.
c. It influenced scientific advancement in Germany only, where Gutenberg's press was based.
d. It did not influence science; though texts with scientific knowledge were printed, distribution of these texts was limited.

38. Which statement best describes how Martin Luther's religious Reformation influenced Western civilization?

a. It contributed to the decline of women's and girls' education.
b. It weakened civil authorities in European towns.
c. It contributed to the rise of individualism.
d. It delayed reform within the Catholic Church itself.

39. A woman has $450 in a bank account. She earns 5% interest on her end-of-month balance. How much interest will she earn for the month?

a. $5.00
b. $22.50
c. $427.50
d. $472.50

40. Three children decide to buy a gift for their father. The gift costs $78.00. One child contributes $24.00. The second contributes $15.00 less than the first. How much will the third child have to contribute?

a. $15.00
b. $39.00
c. $45.00
d. $62.00

41. A woman is traveling to a destination 583 km away. If she drives 78 km every hour, how many hours will it take for her to reach her destination?

    a. 2.22
    b. 3.77
    c. 5.11
    d. 7.47

42. A girl scores a 99 on her math test. On her second test, her score drops by 15. On the third test, she scores 5 points higher than she did on her second. What was the girl's score on the third test?

    a. 79
    b. 84
    c. 89
    d. 99

43. A boy has a bag with 26 pieces of candy inside. He eats 8 pieces of candy, then divides the rest evenly between two friends. How many pieces of candy will each friend get?

    a. 7
    b. 9
    c. 11
    d. 13

44. One worker has an office that is 20 feet long. Another has an office that is 6 feet longer. What is the combined length of both offices?

    a. 26 feet
    b. 36 feet
    c. 46 feet
    d. 56 feet

45. If one gallon of paint can paint 3 rooms, how many rooms can be painted with 28 gallons of paint?

    a. 10
    b. 25
    c. 56
    d. 84

46. How did World War II influence American society?

    a. Consumption decreased in postwar American society.
    b. Thousands of people moved to find work in war-related factories.
    c. Racially integrated army units helped desegregate American society.
    d. Japanese-Americans were banned from serving in the U.S. military.

47. How did the Truman Doctrine shape U.S. foreign policy after World War II?

    a. It influenced President Truman's decision to create commissions on civil rights.
    b. It shaped the U.S. role in rebuilding the economies of postwar Europe.
    c. It led the U.S. government to refrain from interfering with the U.S. economy.
    d. It led to U.S. military involvement in countries such as Korea.

48. The United States fought North Vietnam in the 1960s and 1970s primarily to:
    a. spread democracy modeled on the U.S. system.
    b. demonstrate U.S. power to the Soviet Union.
    c. protect U.S. trade interests in Southeast Asia.
    d. prevent the spread of communism.

49. European colonization of present-day Pennsylvania in the late 17ᵗʰ century is most closely associated with:
    a. the desire for freedom of the press.
    b. escape from high taxes.
    c. the desire for religious freedom.
    d. escape from trade restrictions.

50. Which of the following is a significant structural similarity between the government of the Iroquois Confederacy and the government of the United States?
    a. Many decisions require compromise between two separate entities. In the Iroquois Confederacy, those entities were two different sets of Lords; in the U.S. government, those entities are the House of Representatives and the Senate.
    b. A single leader has significant executive powers: in the Iroquois Confederacy, a chief, and in the U.S. government, the president.
    c. The level of representation in at least one legislative body depended on population. In the Iroquois Confederacy, the population of tribes partially determined representation, and in the United States, the population of states partially determines representation.
    d. A third judicial branch served as a check on the executive power in both the Iroquois Confederacy and the U.S. government.

51. One of the earliest political parties in the United States was the Federalist Party. Its decline is best explained by:
    a. a failure to organize state political parties.
    b. the enmity of wealthy Americans.
    c. its opposition to the War of 1812.
    d. its advocacy of a strong central government.

52. Which of the following is the most significant justification for United States expansion as advocated by the Manifest Destiny?
    a. It was the duty of the United States to spread democracy.
    b. The United States would spread material wealth.
    c. It was the duty of the United States to prevent the spread of slavery.
    d. The United States would spread religious freedom.

53. After the Civil War, President Andrew Johnson disagreed with Congress over Reconstruction policies. Which action by President Johnson best describes the grounds for which he was impeached?
    a. He dismissed a Cabinet member without congressional permission.
    b. He refused to enforce the Fourteenth Amendment.
    c. He sought to disenfranchise former Confederate officers.
    d. He violated Constitution law in forming a third political party.

54. Which of the following is NOT considered a function of management?

    a. Planning
    b. Organizing
    c. Leading
    d. Achieving

55. Which of the following is a problem with the Utilitarian ethical framework?

    a. It focuses only on the means rather than the ends.
    b. It violates people's freedom of speech.
    c. It is arbitrary.
    d. It assumes profit optimization leads to the greatest social benefit.

56. Which of the following is the principle that describes the assumption that systems wear down unless they import energy to reverse this tendency?

    a. Negative entropy
    b. Positive entropy
    c. Positive feedback
    d. Negative feedback

57. Which of the following terms refers to the number of subordinates reporting to one manager?

    a. Staff
    b. Flat structure
    c. Functional structure
    d. Span of management

58. Which of the following theories of motivation is based on the premise that inequity is motivating?

    a. Expectancy theory
    b. Acquired Need theory
    c. Reinforcement theory
    d. Equity theory

59. Which of the following is the correct order of stages through which all groups typically go?

    a. Form, norm, storm, perform, adjourn
    b. Form, storm, perform, norm, adjourn
    c. Form, norm, perform, storm, adjourn
    d. Form, storm, norm, perform, adjourn

60. Which of the following is the term for someone appointed to a group to argue against the group's position in an attempt to avoid groupthink?

    a. Outsider
    b. Devil's advocate
    c. Mind-guard
    d. Leader

English Expression

DIRECTIONS: In the passages that follow, words and phrases are underlined and numbered. Read the alternate suggestions for each underlined part and choose the one that seems to work best with the style and tone of the article and is grammatically correct. The original response is always listed as the first option. Read each passage through before reviewing the questions and responses.

Questions 1-10 pertain to the following excerpt of four paragraphs:

The construction of the Panama Canal began on (1) <u>May 4 1904</u>. The efforts leading up to the start of the canal had been marked by time-consuming frustration and political disagreements. In June of 1902, the United States had begun looking more seriously into a canal across Panama. It was not until January of 1903 that the Hay-Herran Treaty passed, (2) <u>gave</u> the United States government the opportunity to proceed in building the canal.

As it turned out, the process rapidly became complicated. In 1903, Panama was a (3) <u>province of Columbia and while the United States Senate</u> ratified the Hay-Herran Treaty, the Senate of Columbia did not. The debate over the canal also coincided with the Panamanian hopes for (4) <u>independence from Columbia, when Columbian troops</u> tried to block a Panamanian revolt the United States (5) <u>lended</u> its aid. Panama declared independence on November 3rd of 1903. Three days later, the United States signed Hay-Bunau-Varilla Treaty with Panama to begin work on the canal.

Even still, the canal construction experienced delays. The liaison between the United States and Panama was Phillipe Bunau-Varilla, the ambassador who signed the treaty in favor of the canal. (6) <u>Bunau-Varilla though representing Panama was actually a French citizen</u> and thus not eligible to sign treaties on behalf of the Panamanian government. The result was (7) <u>further</u> delays.

Finally, in May of 1904, the United States was cleared to start construction on the canal. Under the advice of engineer John Frank Stevens, the United States utilized a system of dams and locks that would even water levels and make ship passage (8) <u>more easier</u>. (9) <u>As a result</u>, Stevens insisted on housing workers in suitable homes and providing (10) <u>both sanitation and pest control</u>. President Roosevelt would later melt down machinery from work on the canal and have it cast into medals for those who spent at least two years working on the Panama Canal project.

1.
   a. May 4 1904
   b. May 4, 1904
   c. May, 4, 1904
   d. May 4th 1904

2.
   a. gave
   b. was given
   c. giving
   d. have given

3.

    a. province of Columbia and while the United States Senate
    b. province of Columbia yet while the United States Senate
    c. province of Columbia, and while the United States Senate
    d. province of Columbia, and the United States Senate

4.

    a. independence from Columbia, when Columbian troops
    b. independence from Columbia; when Columbian troops
    c. independence from Columbia, but Columbian troops
    d. independence from Columbia. Columbian troops

5.

    a. lended
    b. was lending
    c. lent
    d. had lent

6.

    a. Bunau-Varilla though representing Panama was actually a French citizen
    b. Bunau-Varilla, a French citizen, represented Panama
    c. Bunau-Varilla represented Panama and was actually a French citizen
    d. Bunau-Varilla, though representing Panama, was actually a French citizen

7.

    a. further
    b. farther
    c. furthest
    d. more far

8.

    a. more easier
    b. easier
    c. easy
    d. more easily

9.

    a. As a result
    b. Additionally
    c. Consequently
    d. On the other hand

10.

    a. both sanitation and pest control
    b. both sanitation, and pest control
    c. both sanitation; and pest control
    d. both: sanitation and pest control

Questions 11-20 pertain to the following excerpt of four paragraphs:

The process of creating the United States government, as contained within the Constitution, occurred in a (11) <u>series of steps. Each of which involved debate and compromise</u>. One early issue was that of deciding how many legislative houses to establish under the new Constitution. The Articles of Confederation had provided for a (12) <u>unicameral legislature that is a legislature of one house</u>. Delegates had to debate whether or not this was sufficient for the (13) <u>new government and in May of 1787 delegates from each state</u> arrived in Philadelphia to discuss the issue.

On May 29, 1787, Virginia delegate and then-governor Edmund Randolph proposed what became known as the Virginia Plan. The Virginia Plan, (14) <u>which was drafted by James Madison, later the writer of the Constitution, recommended</u> a bicameral legislative structure with two houses. Within each house, the number of representatives would reflect the population of each state. (15) <u>On the other hand</u>, states with a larger population would have more representatives than states with a smaller population. The reasoning followed that the representatives were responsible for being the voice of their constituents, and states with a larger population had more constituents in need of a voice.

Perhaps not surprisingly, the smaller states objected to the Virginia Plan. They were concerned they any voice they had in Congress would be drowned out by larger states. Add to this a growing North-South divide, and (16) <u>small northern states like Delaware resented the votes that large southern states like Virginia</u> would have. In response, New Jersey delegate William Paterson proposed the New Jersey Plan on June 15, 1787. Under this plan, the legislature would remain unicameral, as it had been under the Articles, and each state would be given a (17) <u>single, equal voice</u>. Population would not feature in deciding a (18) <u>states</u> voice in Congress.

The result was a compromise. Connecticut delegates Roger Sherman and Oliver Ellsworth proposed the Connecticut Compromise on July 16, 1787. The compromise adopted features of the Virginia Plan for the lower house, later the House of Representatives, and features of the New Jersey Plan for the upper house, or the Senate. (19) <u>Finally</u>, the membership of the House of Representatives is decided by population, while (20) <u>membership in the Senate is allotted equally: two representatives and an equal voice for each state</u>.

11.

    a. series of steps. Each of which involved debate and compromise
    b. series of steps: each of which involved debate and compromise
    c. series of steps; each of which involved debate and compromise
    d. series of steps, each of which involved debate and compromise

12.

    a. unicameral legislature that is a legislature of one house
    b. unicameral legislature, that is a legislature of one house
    c. unicameral legislature. That is, a legislature of one house
    d. unicameral legislature that is, a legislature of one house

13.

    a. new government and in May of 1787 delegates from each state
    b. new government, and in May of 1787 delegates from each state
    c. new government and, in May of 1787 delegates from each state
    d. new government and in May of 1787, delegates from each state

14.

    a. which was drafted by James Madison, later the writer of the Constitution, recommended
    b. which was drafted by James Madison [later the writer of the Constitution] recommended
    c. which was drafted by James Madison (later the writer of the Constitution), recommended
    d. which was drafted by James Madison; he was later the writer of the Constitution and recommended

15.

    a. On the other hand
    b. In other words
    c. Additionally
    d. Nevertheless

16.

    a. small northern states like Delaware resented the votes that large southern states like Virginia
    b. small-northern states like Delaware resented the votes that large-southern states like Virginia
    c. small, northern states like Delaware resented the votes that large, southern states like Virginia
    d. small northern states like Delaware, resented the votes that large southern states like Virginia

17.

    a. single, equal voice
    b. single equal voice
    c. single, more equal voice
    d. single-equal voice

18.

    a. states
    b. states'
    c. state's
    d. "states"

19.

    a. Finally
    b. Beyond this
    c. As a result
    d. In consideration

20.

a. membership in the Senate is allotted equally: two representatives and an equal voice for each state

b. membership in the Senate is allotted equally; two representatives and an equal voice for each state

c. membership in the Senate is allotted equally. Two representatives and an equal voice for each state

d. membership in the Senate is allotted equally two representatives and an equal voice for each state

Questions 21-25 pertain to the following excerpt of two paragraphs:

The Connecticut Compromise may have decided the set-up of the new legislature branch, but the issue of population (21) remained problematic, however. The delegates at the Constitutional Convention found themselves at loggerheads in deciding how to count the many slaves that populated the South. (22) Under the Articles of Confederation the question of taxation per state had come down to a question of population, and Southerners objected to paying higher taxes due to the presence of the slaves (whom they considered property or wealth instead of population). A 1783 amendment to the Articles suggested counting each slave as three-fifths of a non-slave (23) citizen, this amendment failed to pass.

During the 1787 convention in (24) Philadelphia though the delegates decided to resurrect the Three-Fifths Compromise regarding state population and apply it to representation. In states where slaves were owned, the slave population would be counted as three-fifths of the non-slave population, thus providing extra numbers for representation based on the number of slaves. This means that a non-slave population of 1000 would be counted as 1000, while a slave population of 1000 would be counted as 600, or three-fifths of 1000. Despite the fact that slaves were not considered citizens and had no legal rights, their numbers contributed to representation in Congress. While the ethical problems of the Three-Fifths Compromise continue to be debated, delegates in 1787 passed the measure as a (25) much needed balance to one of the issues that divided the states.

21.

a. remained problematic, however

b. remained problematic however

c. remained problematic; however

d. remained problematic

22.

a. Under the Articles of Confederation the question of taxation

b. Under the Articles of Confederation, the question of taxation

c. Under the Articles of Confederation; the question of taxation

d. Under the Articles of Confederation, the question, of taxation

23.

    a. citizen, this amendment failed to pass
    b. citizen, however this amendment failed to pass
    c. citizen. This amendment failed to pass
    d. citizen, while this amendment failed to pass

24.

    a. Philadelphia though the delegates
    b. Philadelphia, though the delegates
    c. Philadelphia though, the delegates
    d. Philadelphia, though, the delegates

25.

    a. much needed
    b. much, needed
    c. much-needed
    d. much/needed

Questions 26-35 pertain to the following excerpt of four paragraphs:

Only thirteen years after the (26) <u>ratification of the Constitution the fledgling United States</u> government faced an unexpected challenge. The election of 1800 pitted increasingly divergent political parties (27) <u>against one another: President John Adams led the Federalist Party</u> against his own Vice President Thomas Jefferson, who was at the head of the growing Republican Party. The Federalists favored a strong centralized government and alliances with the British, while the Republicans favored decentralization and alliances with the French. (28) <u>The two men had little respect for one another, they had been running *against* one another in the election of 1796</u>. So, how did Jefferson end up as Adams's Vice President to begin with? Well, the Constitution had created the opportunity for a problem that the Founders had not really anticipated.

The writers of the Constitution had created the (29) <u>Electoral College system giving each elector the opportunity to cast two votes</u>. The system of "running mates" was not yet in place within the Constitution, so both votes cast were counted as votes (30 <u>for President</u>. The immediate runner-up in the election would then be selected as the Vice President. In a perfect system, the main candidate would select a Vice Presidential candidate (31) <u>who would as everyone hoped and expected receive</u> the second highest number of votes. The electors intended to guarantee the results they preferred by having several electors for each main candidate dropping a few votes for the secondary candidate, thus ensuring the main candidate received the highest number of votes. So, in 1796, John Adams ran alongside Thomas Pinckney, while Thomas Jefferson ran alongside Aaron Burr.

The election did not quite work out as planned. To his delight, Adams received a total of 71 electoral votes. (32) <u>To everyone's surprise however it was not Pinckney</u> who received the second highest number of votes (33) <u>but Thomas Jefferson. Who came in with 68 electoral votes</u>. Much to the frustration of both men, they would be working alongside one another when they had just competed against each other in the election. Given these challenges, Adams's term as President was fraught with a number of problems that he was unable to solve effectively.

In the election of 1800, Jefferson made another attempt at the Presidency, with Adams running again to secure a second term. Due to Adams's struggles in office, (34) <u>Jefferson was the expected winner and he ran again with Aaron Burr</u>. But once again, the problems with the Electoral College voting system revealed themselves. The electors planned to give Jefferson the primary number of votes by having only one of the electors drop his second vote, but when the votes were counted it turned out that Jefferson and Burr were tied. The election was placed in the hands of the House of Representatives, but at the time the House was still composed largely of Federalists from Adams's term in office. The Federalists had to choose between what they viewed as two evils. (35) <u>The result, led intensely by Alexander Hamilton (who disliked both men but had even greater dislike for Burr), was an election in favor of Thomas Jefferson</u>.

26.

a. ratification of the Constitution the fledgling United States
b. ratification of the Constitution. The fledgling United States
c. ratification of the constitution, the fledgling United States
d. ratification of the Constitution, the fledgling United States

27.

a. against one another: President John Adams led the Federalist Party
b. against one another. President John Adams led the Federalist Party
c. against one another, President John Adams led the Federalist Party
d. against one another, and President John Adams led the Federalist Party

28.

a. The two men had little respect for one another, they had been running *against* one another in the election of 1796
b. The two men had little respect for one another, had been running against one another in the election of 1796
c. The two men had little respect for one another and had been running against one another in the election of 1796
d. The two men had little respect for one another; had been running against one another in the election of 1796

29.

a. Electoral College system giving each elector the opportunity to cast two votes
b. Electoral College system, giving each elector the opportunity to cast two votes
c. Electoral College system. Each elector cast two votes
d. Electoral College system: giving each elector the opportunity to cast two votes

30.

a. for President
b. for president
c. for the president
d. for: President

31.

    a. who would as everyone hoped and expected receive
    b. who would; as everyone hoped and expected; receive
    c. who would (as everyone hoped and expected) receive
    d. who would receive as everyone hope and expected

32.

    a. To everyone's surprise however it was not Pinckney
    b. To everyone's surprise, however it was not Pinckney
    c. To everyone's surprise however, it was not Pinckney
    d. To everyone's surprise, however, it was not Pinckney

33.

    a. but Thomas Jefferson. Who came in with 68 electoral votes
    b. but Thomas Jefferson; who came in with 68 electoral votes
    c. but Thomas Jefferson: who came in with 68 electoral votes
    d. but Thomas Jefferson, who came in with 68 electoral votes

34.

    a. Jefferson was the expected winner and he ran again with Aaron Burr
    b. Jefferson was the expected winner, and he ran again with Aaron Burr
    c. Jefferson was the expected winner who ran again with Aaron Burr
    d. Jefferson was the expected winner, he ran again with Aaron Burr

35.

    a. The result, led intensely by Alexander Hamilton (who disliked both men but had even greater dislike for Burr) was an election in favor of Thomas Jefferson
    b. The result, led intensely by Alexander Hamilton, who disliked both men but had even greater dislike for Burr, was an election in favor of Thomas Jefferson
    c. The result, led intensely by Alexander Hamilton (who disliked both men but had even greater dislike for Burr), was an election in favor of Thomas Jefferson
    d. The result, led intensely by Alexander Hamilton who disliked both men, but had even great dislike for Burr was an election in favor of Thomas Jefferson

Questions 36-45 pertain to the following excerpt of four paragraphs:

In October of 1800, Spain quietly signed the Third Treaty of San Ildefonso (36) <u>with France, the terms of which required that Spain return the Louisiana Territory to France</u>. Shortly thereafter, the newly elected President Thomas Jefferson (37) <u>got wind of the transfer, and began considering the possibility</u> of purchasing the rights to New Orleans from France. Jefferson sent United States Minister Robert Livingstone to Paris to conduct the initial diplomatic conversations with France regarding the possibility of such a transaction.

The President ultimately ended up getting (38) <u>more than he bargained for – in several ways</u>. Jefferson's primary concern was for the United States to maintain its rights to navigate the Mississippi River and conduct business in the Port of New Orleans. (39) <u>Consequently</u>, Jefferson did not want his country to be drawn into the Napoleonic Wars that were raging (40) <u>across Europe. Although he did not mind taking advantage</u> of any European nations' plans to dispose of New World colonies.

For two years, Jefferson kept his friend and emissary Pierre Samuel du Pont de Nemours in talks with the French government to maintain an ongoing discussion about New Orleans. It was du Pont who suggested in 1802 that the United States consider purchasing the entire territory from France.

From the first, Jefferson was uncomfortable with the idea. For one, Jefferson was disinclined to get (41) <u>in between Spain and France, the Third Treaty of San Ildefonso did not complete the transfer</u> of the Louisiana Territory to France until 1803. More importantly, however, Jefferson was a strict Constitutionalist, and he did not believe the Constitution gave the President the right to complete such a transaction. Jefferson was also concerned about the imbalance of power that would result from the addition of Louisiana. The territory would more than double the size of the United States, giving the federal government power (42) <u>over an expansive territory, and immediately reducing</u> the power that (43) <u>the states' currently held</u>.

Still, the idea remained a distant consideration. In April of 1803, future President James Monroe joined Robert Livingston in Paris to complete the purchase of New Orleans. The two men were authorized to pay up to $10 million for the rights to the city. Much to their shock, Napoleon's Minister of the Treasury offered them the entire Louisiana Territory – include New Orleans, of course – for only $15 million. Monroe and Livingston had (44) <u>no official authorization beyond the purchase of New Orleans but were unwilling to let that deal fall through</u>. As a result, they decided to sign the treaty and pay the money for the full territory, a decision that Jefferson ultimately approved. (45) <u>It is ironic that Jefferson, the most Constitutional of Presidents, is credited</u> with stepping so far outside its boundaries, but few can fault him: in purchasing the Louisiana Territory for $15 million, the United States paid less than three cents per acre.

36.

a. with France, the terms of which required that Spain return the Louisiana Territory to France
b. with France; the terms of which required that Spain return the Louisiana Territory to France
c. with France: the terms of which required that Spain return the Louisiana Territory to France
d. with France, and the terms of which required that Spain return the Louisiana Territory to France

37.

a. got wind of the transfer, and began considering the possibility
b. got wind of the transfer and began considering the possibility
c. got wind of the transfer, began considering the possibility
d. got wind of the transfer, he began considering the possibility

38.

a. more than he bargained for – in several ways
b. more than he bargained for: in several ways
c. more than he bargained for. In several ways
d. more than he bargained for (in several ways)

39.

    a. Consequently
    b. In consideration
    c. At the same time
    d. Incredibly

40.

    a. across Europe. Although he did not mind taking advantage
    b. across Europe; although he did not mind taking advantage
    c. across Europe, although he did not mind taking advantage
    d. across Europe, he did not mind taking advantage

41.

    a. in between Spain and France, the Third Treaty of San Ildefonso did not complete the transfer
    b. in between Spain and France, and the Third Treat of San Ildefonso did not complete the transfer
    c. in between Spain and France, but the Third Treaty of San Ildefonso did not complete the transfer
    d. in between Spain and France, because the Third Treaty of San Ildefonso did not complete the transfer

42.

    a. over an expansive territory, and immediately reducing
    b. over an expansive territory and immediately reducing
    c. over an expansive territory, immediately reducing
    d. over an expansive territory yet immediately reducing

43.

    a. the states' currently held
    b. the state's currently held
    c. the states currently held
    d. the state currently held

44.

    a. no official authorization beyond the purchase of New Orleans but were unwilling to let that deal fall through
    b. no official authorization beyond the purchase of New Orleans; but were unwilling to let that deal fall through
    c. no official authorization beyond the purchase of New Orleans. But were unwilling to let that deal fall through
    d. no official authorization beyond the purchase of New Orleans but they were unwilling to let that deal fall through

45.

    a. It is ironic that Jefferson, the most Constitutional of Presidents, is credited
    b. It is ironic that Jefferson the most Constitutional of Presidents is credited
    c. It is ironic that Jefferson the most Constitutional of Presidents, is credited
    d. It is ironic that Jefferson: the most Constitutional of Presidents, is credited

Questions 46-50 pertain to the following excerpt of two paragraphs:

The purchase of the Louisiana Territory more than doubled the land that composed the United States, but at the time of the purchase the actual amount of land was not entirely known. (46) <u>On the other hand</u>, President Thomas Jefferson was not sure how much land the United States had just bought, and France was not sure how much land it had just sold. To learn more about the Louisiana Territory, President Jefferson commissioned an expedition that would take the explorers all the way to the West Coast. The Louisiana Territory actually stopped at modern-day Montana, but (47) <u>the Pacific Northwest was unclaimed territory at the time, Jefferson sent the Corps of Discovery</u> through that region and to the very shores of the Pacific Ocean.

At the helm of the expedition was (48) <u>Captain Meriwether Lewis, a captain in the United States Army and a personal friend of President Jefferson</u>. Lewis chose his former Army Lieutenant William Clark to accompany him, and the two left (49) <u>Pittsburgh, Pennsylvania,</u> with a team of 31 others in August of 1803. In November of 1805, the expedition reached the mouth of the Columbia River, which feeds into the Pacific Ocean, and spent the winter in the newly constructed Fort Clatsop on the site of modern-day Astoria, Oregon. In March of 1806, Lewis and Clark began the journey home. In August of the same year, (50) <u>they arrived in St. Louis, Missouri. Their journey complete</u>.

46.

   a. On the other hand
   b. At the same time
   c. What is more
   d. In other words

47.

   a. the Pacific Northwest was unclaimed territory at the time, Jefferson sent the Corps of Discovery
   b. the Pacific Northwest was unclaimed territory at the time, but Jefferson sent the Corps of Discovery
   c. the Pacific Northwest was unclaimed territory at the time; Jefferson sent the Corps of Discovery
   d. the Pacific Northwest was unclaimed territory at the time, yet Jefferson sent the Corps of Discovery

48.

   a. Captain Meriwether Lewis, a captain in the United States Army and a personal friend of President Jefferson
   b. Captain Meriwether Lewis a captain in the United States Army and a personal friend of President Jefferson
   c. Captain Meriwether Lewis – a captain in the United States Army and a personal friend of President Jefferson
   d. Captain Meriwether Lewis. Who was a captain in the United States Army and a personal friend of President Jefferson

49.

    a. Pittsburgh, Pennsylvania,
    b. Pittsburg, Pennsylvania
    c. Pittsburg Pennsylvania
    d. Pittsburgh (Pennsylvania)

50.

    a. they arrived in St. Louis, Missouri. Their journey complete
    b. they arrived in St. Louis, Missouri; their journey complete
    c. they arrived in St. Louis, Missouri their journey complete
    d. they arrived in St. Louis, Missouri, their journey complete

Questions 51-60 pertain to the following excerpt of four paragraphs:

The question of (51) <u>womens'</u> suffrage was featured often in American history, but the issue became increasingly important in the mid-19th century. Women began taking on more roles and responsibilities within society, particularly in the Western territories. In 1869, the women in Wyoming petitioned the territory's legislature to grant them the right to vote. At the head of the movement in Wyoming was Esther Morris, six feet tall and the first woman in history to serve as a justice of the peace. She held parties (52) <u>at her home. Where she discussed the issue</u> with the candidates from both political parties.

Each candidate agreed to support a bill for women's suffrage. In November of 1869, (53) <u>the winner Colonel William H. Bright, sent the bill</u> before the Wyoming legislature. Territory Governor John Campbell approved it, and Wyoming gave women the right to vote. According to tradition, (54) <u>70-year-old Louisa Ann Swain</u> became the first woman in America to cast her vote. Almost twenty years later, Wyoming was on the cusp of statehood, but federal congressmen raised the issue of the women voters as a concern for the territory joining the Union. The women of Wyoming actually encouraged the legislature to drop the law so as not to prevent Wyoming's chances. (55) <u>The legislature declined, and responded to Congress</u> that it would enter the Union with its women voters or not at all.

The women's suffrage movement was proceeding somewhat more slowly (56) <u>in the east</u>. Susan B. Anthony and her fellow suffragettes formed the National Woman Suffrage Association in 1869, just after black men in the United States had been given the right to vote. The 15th Amendment had recognized that voting rights identified black men as citizens. The women questioned what their citizenship rights were. (57) <u>If they could not vote, did that mean they were not citizens.</u> The government assured women that they had citizenship through the voting rights of their husbands and fathers. (58) <u>But, for many women this was not enough.</u>

Women pointed out that the restriction of voting rights was inconsistent with the burdens placed on them. Women could not serve on juries, but (59) <u>they could be convicted by a jury – a jury composed entirely of men</u>, that is. Women could be taxed as individuals, even though they were not officially represented in Congress. Nationwide rights for women voters would ultimately have to wait until 1920, (60) <u>when Congress passed the 19th Amendment: and all United States</u> citizens were granted the right to vote, regardless of race or gender.

51.

    a. women'

    b. women's

    c. womans'

    d. women

52.

    a. at her home. Where she discussed the issue

    b. at her home: where she discussed the issue

    c. at her home; where she discussed the issue

    d. at her home, where she discussed the issue

53.

    a. the winner Colonel William H. Bright, sent the bill

    b. the winner, Colonel William H. Bright sent the bill

    c. the winner, Colonel William H. Bright, sent the bill

    d. the winner – Colonel William H. Bright – sent the bill

54.

    a. 70-year-old Louisa Ann Swain

    b. 70-year old Louisa Ann Swain

    c. 70 year-old Louisa Ann Swain

    d. 70 year old Louisa Ann Swain

55.

    a. The legislature declined, and responded to Congress

    b. The legislature declined; and responded to Congress

    c. The legislature declined, responded to Congress

    d. The legislature declined and responded to Congress

56.

    a. in the east

    b. in the: east

    c. in the East

    d. in, the East

57.

    a. If they could not vote, did that mean they were not citizens.

    b. If they could not vote, did that mean they were not citizens?

    c. If they could not vote did that mean they were not citizens.

    d. If they could not vote, that meant they were not citizens.

58.

    a. But, for many women this was not enough.

    b. But for many women this was not enough.

    c. But for many women; this was not enough.

    d. But, for many women this was not enough!

59.

    a. they could be convicted by a jury – a jury composed entirely of men
    b. they could be convicted by a jury: a jury composed entirely of men
    c. they could be convicted by a jury; a jury composed entirely of men
    d. they could be convicted by a jury composed entirely of men

60.

    a. when Congress passed the 19ᵗʰ Amendment: and all United States
    b. when Congress passed the 19th Amendment: and all United States'
    c. when Congress passed the 19th Amendment, and all United States
    d. when Congress passed the 19th Amendment, all United States

Questions 61-70 pertain to the following excerpt of four paragraphs:

Labor laws were slow to change in the United States, and when it came to regulations for labor safety, the employee was often not the priority. It took a series of accidents to prompt regulatory changes that would ensure workplace safety for employees. (61) <u>The most notorious of these accidents were</u> the (62) <u>Triangle Shirtwaist Factory fire, that occurred in March of 1911</u>. As a result of this incident, 146 workers, all young women, perished. (63) <u>The Triangle Shirtwaist fire horrified, and outraged American society</u>, and it initiated a succession of changes that would improve labor laws for all workers in the United States.

In many ways, the Triangle Shirtwaist Factory was not unusual among American businesses, (64) <u>nor were it's business practices unique</u>. The owners, Max Blanck and Isaac Harris, employed mostly women, the majority of whom were immigrants, to ensure that they could pay their employees lower wages. These workers specialized in making shirtwaists, or blouses for women. Like most business owners, Blanck and Harris were wary of their workers and did not trust them to follow the required work schedule, so they locked the workers into the rooms during work hours. Employees were not allowed to leave the building (65) <u>during work hours: except for approved breaks</u>.

Fire was always a concern, so cigarettes were strictly forbidden in the workrooms. (66) <u>Workers often sneaked them in</u>, and historians now agree that this is what happened on that fateful day in 1911. One of the workrooms caught on fire, and workers scrambled to exit the building as the fire began spreading from one floor to another. Blanck and Harris, who had their children visiting with them that day, left the building as soon as the cry of fire rang out. (67) <u>Likewise</u>, many of the workers remained locked in the rooms. The women crowded on the fire escape, (68) <u>which collapsed under the weight, others fell or leaped from the ninth floor</u> of the building. Those on the street watched in horror, helpless to assist the desperate workers who were trapped in the raging flames.

The tragic results of the fire led to necessary changes in workplace safety. The decade-old International Ladies' Garment Workers' Union encouraged solidarity among workers across the United States and began demanding improvements in labor safety laws. Investigation revealed the extensive safety failures (69) <u>that had caused such immense tragedy: the locked doors prevented workers</u> from escaping from multiple exits, the weak fire escape offered little support for those fleeing fire, and the building was equipped with only 27 buckets of water to combat fire. After

23

the event, the government began enacting legislation that would ultimately lead to the safety measures (70) <u>now required today; such as well-labeled fire escapes</u>, fire-proof stairwells in addition to elevators, and sprinkler systems.

61.

    a. The most notorious of these accidents were
    b. The most notorious of these accidents would have been
    c. The most notorious of these accidents would be
    d. The most notorious of these accidents was

62.

    a. Triangle Shirtwaist Factory fire, that occurred in March of 1911
    b. Triangle Shirtwaist Factory fire that occurred in March of 1911
    c. Triangle Shirtwaist Factory fire, that was occurring in March of 1911
    d. Triangle Shirtwaist Factory fire that occurred in March, of 1911

63.

    a. The Triangle Shirtwaist fire horrified, and outraged American society
    b. The Triangle Shirtwaist fire horrified American society. And it also outraged society
    c. The Triangle Shirtwaist fire horrified and outraged American Society
    d. The Triangle Shirtwaist fire horrified and outraged American society

64.

    a. nor were it's business practices unique
    b. nor were its business practices unique
    c. nor were its' business practices unique
    d. nor were its's business practices unique

65.

    a. during work hours: except for approved breaks
    b. during work hours except for: approved breaks
    c. during work hours, except for approved breaks
    d. during work hours. Except for approved breaks

66.

    a. Workers often sneaked them in
    b. Workers often sneaking them in
    c. Workers often snuck them in
    d. Workers often snucked them in

67.

    a. Likewise
    b. Not surprisingly
    c. However
    d. As a result

68.

    a. which collapsed under the weight, others fell or leaped from the ninth floor
    b. which collapsed under the weight and others fell or leaped from the ninth floor
    c. which collapsed under the weight, while others fell or leaped from the ninth floor
    d. which collapsed under the weight, still others fell or leaped from the ninth floor

69.

    a. that had caused such immense tragedy: the locked doors prevented workers
    b. that had caused such immense tragedy; the locked doors prevented workers
    c. that had caused such immense tragedy. The locked doors prevented workers
    d. that had caused such immense tragedy, and the locked doors prevented workers

70.

    a. now required today; such as well-labeled fire escapes
    b. now required today, such as well-labeled fire escapes
    c. now required today: such as well-labeled fire escapes
    d. now required today. Such as well-labeled fire escapes

Written Essay

You will have 30 minutes to write an essay on an assigned topic. Sample topics are provided below. Choose one.

As you create your essay, you should present and support your point of view. Your writing will be evaluated on the quality of the writing and not on your opinion. A good essay will have an organized structure, clear thesis, and logical supporting details. Ensure that you are presenting your topic in a way that appeals to your target audience. Use clear and appropriate word choice throughout. Ensure that grammar, punctuation, and spelling are correct. Your response can be of any length.

1. There is at present a heated debate over the role of the United States in foreign affairs. Some experts argue that the cost and unintended consequences of American intervention are so great that the United States should simply mind its own business. Others assert that America's economic and political power necessitate foreign intervention, both to protect American interests and human rights. Another group derides these opposing views as condescending to the people of other countries, and suggests that the United States consult with foreign countries before becoming involved in their affairs.

2. According to the author of a recent editorial, most of the problems in the United States are a consequence of the national dependence on oil. Oil consumption is expensive, damaging to the environment, and requires the United States to do business with some unsavory regimes. The United States should therefore impose strict gas-mileage requirements on automobiles, effective immediately. Although this would pose some temporary problems for the economy, in the long run it would be the best solution to American oil addiction.

Answer Key and Explanations

Job Knowledge

1. D: All of these can correctly describe a current definition of the term Latin America because more than one definition of this name can be used. One definition is (a) everywhere in the Americas where Spanish or Portuguese is predominantly spoken; i.e., Mexico, most of Central America and South America, Cuba, the Dominican Republic, and Puerto Rico. This definition is based on the colonial history of the Spanish and Portuguese Empires. A second definition is (b) everywhere in the Americas south of the United States, including the Caribbean. By this definition, many English-speaking countries, such as Jamaica, the Bahamas, Trinidad and Tobago, etc. would be included, as would French-speaking countries such as Haiti, Martinique, Guadeloupe, and French Guiana. This definition places more emphasis on socioeconomic colonial history than on culture. To clarify and avoid what seems an overly simplistic name, the United Nations refers instead to "Latin America and the Caribbean" to define this area. A third definition currently used is (c) everywhere in the Americas where a Latinate (i.e. Latin-based or Romance) language is spoken. This includes Spanish, Portuguese, and French. (Note: Romanian is also a Romance language, but many people tend to forget this.) Although French is spoken in Québec, nobody refers to it as part of Latin America because it is considered such an integral part of Canada. In this definition, anywhere creole languages based on Spanish, Portuguese, or French are spoken also is included.

2. D: All of the developments listed occurred during the Early Modern Period. Once scientists had discovered and begun to use the Scientific Method to discover information about a subject under investigation during the Renaissance, scientists began to use principles of the Scientific Method, such as proof by empirical evidence, to conduct experiments (a) during the Early Modern Period. Multinational empires gave way to developing nation-states (b) which were then authoritarian and which eventually became modern nations. In addition, technology progressed more rapidly (c) during this time. Transportation and communication improved, thereby allowing more intercultural contact, colonization, and globalization.

3. C: The Connecticut Compromise was the plan that finally determined how the states would be represented in the government. During the Constitutional Convention or Philadelphia Convention, delegates drafting the Constitution disagreed on this point. The Virginia Plan (a), proposed by the Virginia delegation based on James Madison's ideas, held that states should be represented in proportion to their population sizes. Accordingly, the Virginia Plan was called the "large states plan." William Paterson proposed the New Jersey Plan (b). The New Jersey delegation objected to the Virginia Plan, as proportional representation could give unfair advantages to bigger states like Virginia and crowd out smaller states like New Jersey. The New Jersey Plan was called the "small states plan." It was rejected by the convention but helped small states have their point heard. The Plan of Charles Pinckney (d) of South Carolina has fewer recorded details as Pinckney did not present a written copy, and only James Madison's notes about it remain. The Convention did not debate Pinckney's plan. The Connecticut Compromise (c), proposed by Robert Sherman, reached a balance between large and small states by stipulating the House would be represented in proportion to the states' populations while the Senate would have one vote per state. This combined elements of both the Virginia/large states and New Jersey/small states plans. It took delegates 42 days to agree to this conclusion, but the Connecticut Compromise finally resolved the issue of state representation.

4. B: It is not true about the U.S. Constitution that its first thirteen amendments make up the Bill of Rights. The Bill of Rights consists of the first TEN amendments to the Constitution. Furthermore, the United States Constitution is actually both the oldest (a) and the shortest (c) written constitution still used by any country in the world today. The Constitution replaced the Articles of Confederation after a period of six years (d). The Articles of Confederation were ratified in 1781, and the Constitution was ratified in 1787.

5. D: None of these statements is correct regarding U.S. political parties. The Democratic and Republican Parties have not been the two main parties since 1787 (a); instead, these parties have been the two main parties since the General Election of 1856. 1787 was the year that the U. S. Constitution was ratified. The Democratic Party was not founded in 1854 (b) but in 1824. The Republican Party was not founded in 1824 (c) but in 1854.

6. D: Having a standing army and navy does not embody a principle of Jeffersonian Democracy. Thomas Jefferson believed that having standing armed forces was dangerous as it threatened our liberty. He felt that economic strategies such as embargos were safer and more effective means of coercion if necessary. Jefferson did hold that the representation of the people was the central political value of American Democracy (a). He maintained that separation of church and state (b) was the best way to keep the government free from religious disagreements and reciprocally to keep religion free from interference or corruption by the government. Jefferson believed the federal government must not violate individual rights as expressed in the Bill of Rights, and must not violate states' rights (c) as he wrote in the Kentucky Resolutions and James Madison wrote in the Virginia Resolutions, both in 1798.

7. A: The first American Supreme Court decision ever to strike down a state law as unconstitutional was Fletcher v. Peck (1810). The ruling mandated that the State of Georgia could repeal a corrupt land grant previously made. In the 1803 case of Marbury v. Madison (b), the Supreme Court ruled that it could strike down acts of Congress if it deemed them unconstitutional. In the 1816 case of Martin v. Hunter's Lessee (c), the Supreme Court ruled that Federal courts may review decisions by State courts if they are based on Federal law or the Constitution. In the 1819 case of McCullough v. Maryland (d), the Supreme Court ruled that Maryland could not levy a tax on the Federal bank because state governments cannot impede legitimate actions of the Federal government.

8. B: The first event was immigration of Europeans to America hit a high in 1907, when 1,285,349 European immigrants came to America. The numbers were so great that Congress passed the Emergency Quota Act (a) in 1921. In order to implement greater restrictions on the influx of Southern and Eastern Europeans—particularly Jews, Italians, and Slavs—arriving in larger numbers since the 1890s, and even more as refugees before and during the Nazi and World War II years, Congress further passed the 1924 Immigration Act (c), which prohibited most European refugees from entering the United States. During the Great Depression (d) of the 1930s, immigration declined sharply due to the lack of economic opportunities.

9. C: Claude McKay was the only person in this list who was actually African-American. His landmark sonnet, "If We Must Die," published in 1919, managed to express black defiance against ongoing racist events without ever mentioning race directly. By the end of World War II, McKay's poetry had become a major representation of the realities of contemporary African-American life, along with James Weldon Johnson's novels. Playwright Ridgely Torrence (a) was white. His Three Plays for a Negro Theatre, which premiered in 1917, depicted black people as real and complex human beings in contrast to the traditional stereotypical portrayals of minstrel and blackface theatre. These plays actually helped begin the Harlem Renaissance. Black author James Weldon Johnson described the premiere of Torrence's three plays as "…the most important single event in the entire history of the Negro in the American Theatre." Carl van Vechten (b) was also white. He was an important patron of the arts who helped to further the Harlem Renaissance by funding the works of black artists. He was also a writer and photographer. Many of his portrait photographs are famous, such as one of writer Gertrude Stein in 1934, one of Harlem Renaissance poet Langston Hughes in 1936, a self-portrait photo in 1939, and one of Virgil Thomson in 1947, as well as photo portraits of author James Baldwin, actress Ruby Dee, singers Bessie Smith, Billie Holliday, and Ella Fitzgerald—all Harlem Renaissance artists—as well as portrait photographs of many other American celebrities. He also wrote the controversial novel Nigger Heaven and an essay for Vanity Fair magazine entitled "Negro Blues Singers," both published in 1926. George Gershwin (d), a white Jewish American composer, created the opera Porgy and Bess, an all-black production with black actors playing black characters, still an unusual characteristic when the work was first performed in 1935.

10. D: The decision in Frontiero v. Richardson (1973) did not involve discrimination based on race; instead, it involved discrimination based on sex. The Supreme Court ruled in this case that a statute awarding benefits to the spouses of male members of the uniformed services but not to the spouses of female members of the uniformed services was unconstitutional. The decision in (a) Korematsu v. United States (1944) ruled that American citizens of Japanese ancestry could be interned and denied basic constitutional rights. The decision in (b) Loving v. Virginia (1967) ruled laws banning marriages between different races as unconstitutional. The decision in (c) Jones v. Alfred H. Mayer Co. (1968) ruled that the Federal government can forbid racial discrimination in private housing by the terms of the Civil Rights Act of 1968. The decision in Adarand Constructors, Inc. v. Pena (1995) ruled that racial discrimination, including affirmative action as discrimination in favor of a minority, is subject to strict scrutiny by the courts.

11. C: The United States took the first photos from space and accomplished the first suborbital launch of animals (fruit flies. The photos were taken in 1946 from a modification of a V2 rocket, and the fruit flies were launched in 1947 on a modified V2. The first suborbital launch of any man-made rocket into space (a) was accomplished by the Germans testing their original V2 rocket during World War II. After the war ended, Americans captured German rockets and used them for their own space experiments. They first used a German V2 rocket when they launched it in a cosmic radiation experiment in 1946. Later the same year, Americans took the photographs from another V2 they had altered. The first orbital launch of an unmanned satellite (b) was Sputnik, launched by the Soviets on October 4, 1957. This satellite sent radio signals to Earth and gave data about temperature, pressure, and electron density of the ionosphere. Two months after Sputnik launched, in order to compete with the USSR; the US tried to launch Vanguard 1 into space but was unsuccessful. Less than two months later, the U.S. succeeded in launching Explorer 1 on January 31, 1958. The Soviets accomplished the first launch of a spacecraft into orbit with an animal on board (d) with Laika, a dog, on Sputnik 2 on November 3, 1957.

12. C: Dwight D. Eisenhower was President of the U.S. when the Vietnam War started in 1959 and Gerald Ford was President when it ended in 1975. John F. Kennedy was President from 1961 until his assassination in 1963 and the Vietnam War went on during his entire brief administration; Richard M. Nixon was President from 1969-1974 and did much to bring about the end of the war and the U.S.' involvement in the war, but the war did not end during his administration (a). Following the Paris Peace Accords, American forces withdrew from 1973 to 1975. Harry S. Truman was President before Eisenhower, from 1945-1953, so his administration ended six years before the war began (b). {For Kennedy, see (a).} Dwight D. Eisenhower was President from 1953-1961, so the Vietnam War went on during his entire administration; President Gerald R. Ford was President after Nixon resigned, from 1974-1977, and he announced the end of the Vietnam War and all U.S.

aid on television on April 23, 1975 (c). Saigon fell a week later. Therefore, in answer (d), Eisenhower is correct but Nixon is incorrect.

13. D: What did not occur during the Clinton administration was The House and Senate did not impeach President Clinton for lying about an affair. A majority in the House voted to impeach him for this, but the Senate voted to acquit him of the charges, so he was not impeached. The Clinton administration did experience a long period of economic expansion (a). This expansion was due in part to the internet bubble, which created many more jobs. First Lady Hillary Clinton succeeded in getting the Children's Health Insurance Program (CHIP) passed (b). This was the only success within President and Mrs. Clinton's efforts to legislate universal healthcare. They worked on their program for two years, but it met with too much resistance from special interests to succeed (c). During the Clinton years, there were terrorist attacks by both radical Muslim groups such as Al-Qaeda and by Americans. A Kuwaiti terrorist set off explosives in the basement of One World Trade Center, killing six people and injuring thousands, in 1993. In 2000, millennium attack plots included an attempted bombing at the Los Angeles airport and other attempts. Two Americans, Timothy McVeigh and Terry Nichols, were responsible for bombing the Alfred P. Murrah Federal Building in Oklahoma City in 1995. 168 people died in the Oklahoma explosion. At that time, the Oklahoma City bombing was the largest terrorist attack on U.S. land since World War II.

14. A: There was not less immigration to the U.S. from 2000-2005 than in other years. In fact, more immigration to the U.S. occurred in these five years than in any other five-year period of U.S. history (b). It is true that borders were more secure following the terrorist attacks of 9/11/2001 (c). However, despite increased security measures, almost eight million people immigrated to the U.S. (d).

15. D: The amendment that is included in the Bill of Rights, which consists of the first ten amendments to the Constitution, is the Tenth Amendment. It states that all powers not specified as powers of the federal government are powers that the states keep (1791). The amendment that states cannot be sued by individuals (a) is the Eleventh Amendment (1798). The amendment abolishing slavery (b) is the Thirteenth Amendment (1865). The amendment for the direct election of senators (c) is the Seventeenth Amendment (1913).

16. B: Only the federal government has the power to give copyrights and patents to individuals or companies. The power to levy taxes, borrow money, and spend money (a) is a power shared by federal and state governments. The power to set the criteria that qualify individuals to vote (c) is a power given to state governments only. The power to ratify amendments proposed to the Constitution (d) is a power of only the state governments.

17. A: The action that needs a three-fourths majority vote is state approval of a proposed constitutional amendment. Proposing a constitutional amendment (b) requires a two-thirds majority vote. Ratifying presidential appointments in the Senate (c) also requires a two-thirds majority vote. Introducing charges for impeachment in the House of Representatives (d) requires a simple majority vote.

18. A: By 1840, more than one third of all Americans lived west of the Alleghenies, but not two thirds. It is correct that in the first half of the 19th century, the American population doubled every 25 years (b). It is also correct that westward expansion increased as more people moved west (c) during these years. It is correct that there was not a lot of immigration to the U.S. from other countries before 1820 (d).

19. B: China' production of an atomic bomb in 1964. The USSR launched *Sputnik* (a), the first man-made satellite, into space in 1957. The USSR detonated a hydrogen bomb (c) in 1953, the year after the US detonated its first hydrogen bomb (d) in 1952.

20. D: The action least associated with Reagan's anti-Communist measures was (d), his withdrawal of Cuban troops from Angola in 1988. This troop withdrawal was in answer to pressure to force an end to South Africa's apartheid policies, which segregated blacks from whites. The US levied economic sanctions against South Africa in 1986, after "constructive engagement" efforts failed to end apartheid. In 1988, the Reagan administration negotiated to allow black majority rule in Namibia and to remove Cuban troops from Angola. Therefore answer (d) is a reflection of anti-apartheid actions rather than anti-Communist actions. In efforts to protect the US from Communism, Reagan reinforced our systems of military weaponry (a). He introduced the Strategic Defense Initiative to establish antimissile systems in space (b). In addition, he announced his "Reagan Doctrine," which granted American support to freedom fighters who resisted communist rule (c).

21. D: All of these were actions taken by the Bush administration between 1989-1992, is correct. In 1991, the US and Russia signed the START I treaty, and in 1992, they signed the START II treaty (a). Both of these treaties were agreements by both countries to decrease their arsenals of nuclear weapons. In 1989, the US invaded Panama and overthrew Dictator Manuel Noriega while supporting the National Opposition Union there, which won the 1990 election against the Sandinista Front; and in 1992, US diplomacy ended the civil war in El Salvador (b). Also in 1992, the US signed the North American Free Trade Agreement (NAFTA) with Canada and Mexico, and the US Senate ratified it in 1994, (c). This agreement provided for trading relations among these countries that were mostly free of tariffs. The Persian Gulf War resulted from Iraq's invasion of Kuwait in 1990. Bush intervened with the US Air Force in January of 1991, and within a month he mobilized the Army, Marine Corps, Navy, and Coast Guard to Saudi Arabia, subsequently invading Iraq. At Bush's encouragement, other countries also sent troops there. These combined forces moved the Iraqis out of Kuwait in four days. The UN Security Council approved a cease-fire in April 1991; a hundred days after the ground forces were deployed. Additional actions by Bush during this period included sending troops to Somalia in 1992 to manage the distribution of humanitarian aid and assigning a UN peacekeeping force in 1993 to assume this duty.

22. C: The person or group *not* instrumental in advancing civil rights and desegregation after WWII was (c), Congress. As African American soldiers came home from the war, racial discord increased. President Harry Truman (a) appointed a Presidential Committee on Civil Rights in 1946. This committee published a report recommending that segregation and lynching be outlawed by the federal government. However, Congress ignored this report and took no action. Truman then used his presidential powers to enforce desegregation of the military and policies of "fair employment" in federal civil service jobs. The National Association for the Advancement of Colored People (NAACP) (d) brought lawsuits against racist and discriminatory practices, and in resolving these suits, the Supreme Court (b) further eroded segregation. For example, the Supreme Court ruled that primaries allowing only whites would be illegal, and it ended the segregation of interstate bus lines.

23. B: Bill Clinton did not receive 47% of the votes but 43.2%, while George Bush received not 35% but 37.7% of the votes. In other words, this was a close election. Although Bush's actions to resolve the Persian Gulf War did earn him high public approval ratings (a), problems with the economy in America weakened his bid for reelection (c). Arkansas Governor Bill Clinton's campaign focusing on his views as a more moderate, less liberal, Democrat appealed to voters (d). Another factor that detracted from Bush's campaign was the third-party candidacy of H.

24. C: It is not true that Congress rejected Clinton's health care proposal wholesale (c). Although his motion for universal coverage was denied by Congress, some parts of Clinton's proposal were passed into law, such as the Children's Health Insurance Program (CHIP).

Clinton announced in 1993 that he would suspend the ban on gays in the military. However, due to objections by antigay interests, Clinton changed his policy and reached an agreement with Congress such that military management could not question personnel regarding sexual orientation, and service persons could not offer any information on the subject—the "don't ask-don't tell" policy (a). In 1993, Clinton's administration passed the Family and Medical Leave Act, which required most companies with at least 50 employees to give employees up to 12 weeks of unpaid leave for family bonding and/or to care for an immediate family member who is ill. The act also requires employers to maintain health benefits during that leave. . As the federal deficit continued to grow, Clinton made a financial plan that included raising taxes and lowering federal spending by cutting government jobs and other means. The plan was narrowly passed by Congress (d).

25. B: The "Brady Bill" passed without opposition, is not correct. When John Hinckley Jr. tried to assassinate President Reagan in1981, he failed, but he severely wounded James Brady, Reagan's Press Secretary, who was riding with him. Brady almost died and suffered permanent disabilities. When the Brady Handgun Violence Prevention Act (1993) was proposed, the National Rifle Association (NRA) lobbied vigorously against it. However, Congress passed the bill over this powerful group's objections. This law mandated a five-day waiting period before a person could buy a handgun (a) and allocated funds towards the design of a computer system that could more quickly and efficiently run background checks (c). Additional crime control legislation proposed by the Clinton administration included a 1994 bill that allocated more than $8 billion to hire an additional 100 000 police officers (d).

26. D: All of these factors helped the Republicans gain control of both the House and the Senate in 1994 during Clinton's administration. Allegations regarding the President's character, specifically involvement in the Whitewater Development Corporation scandal and allegations of inappropriate sexual advances made by Clinton during his gubernatorial tenure, (a) and (b) were factors that weakened the Democratic position. Additionally, disagreements regarding healthcare legislation and gays in the military (c) further weakened the President's credibility and strengthened the Republican position.

27. C: The Senate never voted to impeach Clinton. The grounds for impeachment were perjury and obstruction of justice (a) based upon Clinton's denial of an extramarital relationship with intern Monica Lewinsky. Clinton later admitted to the relationship (d). The House of Representatives voted to impeach the President (b) under the influence of Speaker of the House Newt Gingrich and other Republicans. After a trial in the Senate, the Senate voted against convicting Clinton, and he was acquitted of all charges. Many people agreed with First Lady Hillary Clinton that the entire impeachment episode, regardless of Clinton's actions, was part of a "vast right-wing conspiracy" against Clinton by Republicans, which she stated had gone on since he announced his candidacy for President.

28. D: It is not true that PCs had less impact on businesses than on home users. Businesses had been using mainframe computers since around 1946 (a), after World War II. This use became more frequent as companies found them advantageous to tracking and eventually processing, billing and payroll records. Mainframe computers were so large that they occupied entire rooms. When microprocessors were developed in the 1970s, it became possible to create a much smaller computer, the Personal Computer or PC (b). Due to its much smaller size and price, the PC enabled home computer use for the first time (c).

29. C: The rates of both productivity and inflation in the US was approximately 2% by 2000. By this time, the US economy was not increasing at a rate of 5% a year (a) but of 4% a year. Almost half of industrial growth contributing to economic prosperity was due to the "information revolution" made possible by the invention of the PC. The rate of unemployment in America at this time had not gone down to 6% (b) but to 4.7%. The stock market in the US had not just doubled in six years (d); it had actually quadrupled from 1992-1998 due to the increase in American households that owned stocks or bonds. Most of this ownership resulted from tax law changes regulating retirement accounts.

30. D: It is not true that (d) the Waco siege at the Branch Davidian compound lasted for two weeks. In fact, once the FBI attacked the compound, the resulting siege lasted for 51 days. It is true that the Branch Davidians were a Protestant sect that had split off from the Seventh Day Adventists and lived on a compound near Waco, Texas (a). Following reports of gunfire and weapons caches there, the Bureau of Alcohol, Tobacco and Firearms (ATF) conducted surveillance and obtained a search warrant (b). When ATF attempted to execute the warrant, gunfire was exchanged between the compound and ATF agents, and four agents were killed, whereupon the FBI became involved and attacked the compound (c). Following the 51-day siege, the FBI gassed the main building as Davidians set several fires in the building. Various sources claim the deaths totaled 76-86. One of the fatalities was Branch Davidian leader David Koresh whose original name was Vernon Wayne Howell. Note: Despite videotaped records, there is still much controversy surrounding this event.

31. B: The GATT countries did agree to abolish or decrease many of their tariffs, but this agreement did not include only 57 countries. It was much larger, including a total of 117 countries. The GATT was approved by Congress in 1994 (a). In addition to having 117 countries agree to increase free trade, the GATT also set up the World Trade Organization (WTO) for the purpose of settling any differences among nations related to trade (c). Another instance of free trade policy established in the 1990s was the Senate's ratification of NAFTA. The negotiation of this agreement was originally made by the first Bush administration, with President Bush and the leaders of Canada and Mexico signing it in 1992 (d), but it still needed to be ratified.

32. D: When Gore demanded another recount of votes in Florida during the 2000 election, it yielded the same results, is not true. When Gore demanded another Florida recount, the Supreme Court decided in a vote of 5 to 4 against that recount, so it was not made and there were no more results. It is true that Al Gore did win the majority of popular votes (a). It is also true that votes for Green Party candidate Ralph Nader diverted some votes from Gore (b). Many people admired Nader as a crusader for consumer issues, but there was concern that because he could never attract enough votes to win the election, he would simply hurt Gore's chances by detracting some liberals' votes from Gore. It is true that the electoral vote count from Florida would determine the final outcome of the election (c). It is also true that there was a great deal of confusion in Florida over the way the ballots were designed, the ability of Florida's large population of senior citizen voters to read and fill out the ballots correctly, and whether parts of the ballots had been punched through or not. Controversy also brewed over the numbers of votes, such that the final tally was not even certified until November 27.

33. A: It is not true that the US defeated the Taliban and captured Osama bin Laden shortly after 9/11/2001. Osama bin Laden was killed during a raid on a private compound in Pakistan in 2011, nearly 10 years after the attacks. It is true that Muslim terrorists flew two of the four American airplanes they had hijacked into the twin towers of the World Trade Center in New York City (b). They flew the third of the four planes into the US Department of Defense's headquarters, the Pentagon building in Arlington, Virginia, (c) near Washington, D.C. The fourth plane crashed in a field near Shanksville, Pennsylvania, after some of the passengers on board tried to overtake the

33

terrorists (d). President George W. Bush announced a "war on terrorism" after these attacks killed a total of 2,995 people.

34. C: Under the Western European feudal system, rulers granted vassals land in exchange for military and political service. Although the right to use land would often pass from father to son, it was not on the basis of blood relations that a ruler granted land to a vassal; this eliminates option B. Religious institutions such as monasteries did indeed own land, but did not own most of it, eliminating option A. Finally, feudalism was a land-based economy that made a shift from a spice-based economy to a gold-based economy. Therefore, option D can be eliminated.

35. A: The Catholic Church was both powerful and wealthy in medieval Europe. It affected the lives of both the rich and poor; for example, wealthy families often donated to monasteries in exchange for prayers on the donors' behalf. This eliminates option B. Because of these donations, some monasteries became quite wealthy. Rather than being a neutral force, the Catholic Church wielded political power. In medieval times, some claimed that rulers derived their authority to rule from the Catholic Church itself. These facts eliminate options C D.

36. A: The Crusades' biggest impact upon Europe's Jewish population was that entire Jewish communities were killed during the First Crusade. This is the only option that accurately describes historical effects of the Crusades on the Jewish population. Rather than diminishing anti-Jewish sentiment, the Crusades seemed to inflame it, eliminating option B. One specific example of Crusades-era anti-Semitism is that many Jewish people were excluded from particular trades, and thus did not profit from the Crusades. This fact eliminates option C. Finally, there were no Jewish-only battalions during the Crusades, eliminating option D.

37. B: Johann Gutenberg's printing press led to increased scientific knowledge and advancement as scientific texts were printed and dispersed throughout Europe. Because the distribution of such texts extended outside of Germany, options C and D may be eliminated. Gutenberg Bibles were printed using Gutenberg's press, and thus Gutenberg's invention was likely a factor in the Reformation of the Catholic Church. In fact, Martin Luther's Ninety-Five Theses (against the Catholic Church) were printed using a printing press. However, this reformation occurred alongside, rather than in place of, the advancement of scientific knowledge. This eliminates option A.

38. C: With its emphasis on an individual's relationship with God and personal responsibility for salvation, the religious reformation sparked by Martin Luther in 1517 contributed to a rise in individualism. Rather than weakening the civil authorities in Europe, the Reformation served to strengthen many secular authorities by undermining the authority of the Catholic Church. This eliminates answer B. Although the Reformation deemphasized the Virgin Mary, it influenced improvements to education for women and girls, particularly in Germany. This eliminates answer A. Finally, option D can be rejected because the Catholic Church underwent its own internal reformation, in part due to Luther's Reformation.

39. B: Calculate 5% of $450: $450 * 0.05 = $22.50

This is the amount of interest she will earn.

40. C: First, figure out how much the second child contributed: $24.00 - $15.00 = $9.00

Then, calculate how much the first two children contributed in total: 24 + 9 = $33.00

Finally, figure out how much the third child will have to contribute:
$78.00 - $33.00 = $45.00

41. D: Divide the total distance she must travel (583km) by the number of kilometres she drives each hour (78km) to figure out how many hours it will take to reach her destination:

583 km / 78 km = 7.47 hours

42. C: First, calculate her score on the second test: 99 – 15 = 84

Then, calculate her score on the third test: 84 + 5 = 89

43. B: First, figure out how many pieces of candy are in the bag before they are divided:

26 – 8 = 18

Then, figure out how many pieces each friend will get by dividing by 2: 18 / 2 = 9

44. C: First, calculate the length of the second office: 20 + 6 = 26 feet

Then, add both values together to get a combined length: 26 + 20 = 46 feet

45. D: One gallon of paint can paint three rooms, so to find out how many 28 gallons can do, that number must be multiplied by 3:   28 * 3 = 84 rooms

46. B: Many Americans migrated during World War II, seeking work in war-related factories; boomtowns sprang up as a result. Some Japanese-Americans served in the United States military during World War II; in fact, the all-Japanese 442nd Regimental Combat Team, was decorated by the U.S. government for its service. This eliminates choice D. Answer C can be rejected because Caucasian and African-American soldiers served in segregated units. Answer A can be eliminated because consumption actually increased in postwar American society, as production was high and returning U.S. soldiers had income to spend.

47. D: The Truman Doctrine was intended to prevent Greece and Turkey from becoming communist countries. However, its broad language had implications beyond those two nations, suggesting that U.S. policy generally should be to aid people who resisted outside forces attempting to impose communist rule. This doctrine led to U.S. involvement in Korea and Vietnam, where U.S. forces fought against communist forces in those nations. The United States did have a plan for assisting the European economies, but it was the Marshall Plan, not the Truman Doctrine. This eliminates choice B. While President Truman did establish a President's Committee on Civil Rights, it was not as a result of the Truman Doctrine. This eliminates answer A. Finally, when inflation plagued the postwar U.S. economy, the federal government took measures to address inflation and other economic issues, rather than steering clear of them. This eliminates choice C.

48. D: During the Vietnam War, a central aim of the United States was to prevent the spread of communism. At the time of the war, North Vietnamese communist forces threatened South Vietnam, and the United States came to the aid of the South Vietnamese government. The Domino Theory of communism held that one nation's conversion to communism was likely to lead to other nations in that region also converting to communism. The aim of the United States was essentially negative (to stop communism) rather than positive (to implement a specific kind of democracy). This eliminates option A. Option B and C can both be rejected because neither describes the primary aim of U.S. involvement in Vietnam in the 1960s and 1970s. While A, B, and C could have been incidental benefits obtained by fighting North Vietnam, none correctly state the primary goal of the U.S.

49. C: Pennsylvania is most closely associated with William Penn, a Quaker of the Society of Friends. Penn hoped to establish a colony where Quakers would be free to practice their religion. This colony offered religious tolerance toward many other religions as well; Dutch Mennonites and German Baptists were among those who came to Pennsylvania. The desire for freedom of the press was not a salient concern in the motivation for colonizing Pennsylvania; this eliminates option A. Although some European colonists came to Pennsylvania for economic reasons, these are not best understood in terms of escaping high taxes or trade restrictions. This eliminates options B and D.

50. A: The Iroquois Confederacy was a confederacy of originally five (and later six) Native American Tribes, founded in 1570. Many decisions involved compromise between two sets of Lords from different tribes, analogous to the compromise involved in decision-making between the U.S. House of Representatives and the U.S. Senate. For the Confederacy to accept a decision, Mohawk and Seneca Lords needed to come to an agreement with Oneida and Cayuga Lords. Option B can be rejected because there is no chief in the Iroquois Confederacy analogous to the U.S. President. Option C can be rejected because the Iroquois Confederacy did not involve representation based upon a tribe's population. Option D can be rejected because there was no judicial branch in the Iroquois Confederacy analogous to that of the U.S. government.

51. C: The Federalist Party advocated a pro-British foreign policy and therefore opposed the War of 1812. This made the Federalists unpopular with many Americans; this unpopularity deepened when the war ended with American victory. The Federalist Party did advocate a strong central government; however, this position was not a key factor in the Party's decline. This eliminates option D. Option A can be rejected because the Federalist Party did organize state political parties in states such as Connecticut, Delaware, and Maryland. Many members of the Federalist Party were pro-trade and pro-business, as many members were well-to-do businessmen. This eliminates option B.

52. A: Central to the Manifest Destiny (the belief that it was the right and duty of the United States to expand its borders) was the belief that the United States had a duty to spread democracy, offering a democratic example to the rest of the world. Option B was much less significant; proponents of the Manifest Destiny were more interested in spreading what they regarded as civilization than in spreading material prosperity in particular. Option C can be rejected because the issue of slavery was controversial; some proponents of the Manifest Destiny were decided supporters of slavery, and others were not. Option D can be rejected because religious freedom was not a central issue for proponents of Manifest Destiny.

53. A: After a series of disagreements over Reconstruction Policy, Congress passed the Tenure of Office Act, according to which the President needed congressional consent to dismiss from office anyone who had been confirmed by the Senate. President Johnson violated the Act by dismissing Secretary of War Edwin Stanton, whom radical Republicans wanted to keep in office. Congress accordingly impeached President Johnson. Regarding option B, Southern states did enact "Black Laws" to prevent African Americans from voting, but President Johnson was not impeached because he allowed such laws (and thus failed to enforce the Fourteenth Amendment). Johnson did seek to disenfranchise former Confederate officers, and he did attempt to form a third political party; but neither of these actions were grounds for his impeachment (with respect to the former action, radical Republicans were in agreement). This eliminates choices C and D respectively.

54. D: The four functions of management are considered to be: planning (identifying goals and deciding how to achieve them); organizing (defining the relationships in an organization); leading (motivating staff); and controlling (reviewing performance and taking action based on that review). Although managers certainly need to achieve goals and objectives in order to be successful, "achieving" is not a stand-alone function of management.

55. D: A utilitarian approach seeks the greatest good for the greatest number of people. This approach, however, uses company profits as the sole yardstick for measuring what is good, and therefore doesn't reflect the importance of social benefits or costs beyond a company bottom line.

56. A: The term *negative entropy* stands for the idea that all systems eventually wear down and thus need to acquire additional energy to sustain themselves.

57. D: The term *span of management* refers to the number of staff who report to one manager.

58. D: The equity theory posits that employees assess their situations relative to that of their co-workers. It further asserts that if an employee finds an inequity, such as a coworker receiving a raise, the employee will be motivated to resolve that inequity in some way, e.g., by talking to his/her supervisor or finding a different job.

59. D: Groups typically go through the following stages in this order: form, storm (conflict among group members), norm (resolution of conflict), perform (task accomplishment), adjourn.

60. B: To avoid the problems with groupthink, one step a leader can take is to appoint a devil's advocate to argue against the group's position.

English Expression

1. B: Correct punctuation in a date requires a comma between the day of the month and the year. The lack of a comma in the expression of the date (even with the use of "4th") makes the expression incomplete. The comma placement between the month and the day is unnecessary and inaccurate in the expression of the date.

2. C: The word "giving" follows the grammatical structure of the sentence most clearly: "It was not until January of 1903 that the Hay-Herran Treaty passed, *giving* the United States government the opportunity to proceed in building the canal." The word "gave" makes the reading of the sentence awkward without an accompanying conjunction, while the phrases "was given" and "have given" make no sense.

3. C: The comma before the word "while" creates a slight pause in the sentence, signals a coordinating conjunction, and indicates the start of a new independent clause. The lack of the comma creates the potential for a run-on sentence. The use of "yet" is redundant, since the use of "while" to begin the new clause creates the necessary sense of contrast. The removal of the word "while," though not inaccurate, removes some of the impact of the statement.

4. B: Answer choice B avoids the dreaded "comma splice" – that is, a comma that joins two independent clauses. In this case, a semicolon signals the separation of two complete ideas. The conjunction "but" does not offer much to the context of the sentence and actually creates a measure of confusion, and the use of a period without the relative adverb "when" removes some of the sense that is contained within the sentence.

Mometrix

5. C: The word "lent" is correct usage for the past tense of "lend." "Lended" is not a word, while "was lending" and "had lent" make no sense in the sentence.

6. D: The commas offset both sides of the expression "though representing Panama" and create sufficient pause in the reading to establish clarity in the sentence's meaning – a quality that is lacking without commas. The reordering of the words (in answer choice B) alters the context of the sentence unnecessarily. Similarly, the removal of the qualifier "though" also changes the meaning of the sentence for the reader.

7. A: The original option is correct. The use of "further" applies to a more abstract or figurative context (as in this case, with "further delays"), while the use of "farther" is more literal and physical (as in, "Columbia is farther from the U.S. than Panama"). "Furthest" makes little sense in this sentence, and "more far" is almost never correct or necessary.

8. B: The word "easier" is correct usage in this context. "More easier" is never correct. The use of "easy," while not necessarily incorrect, is not the best choice in conveying the meaning of the sentence. And "more easily" is the wrong form of an adverb modifier in this context.

9. B: Question 9 essentially asks for the best transitional expression to open the sentence. In the previous sentence, readers are told that engineer advised the U.S. government to use a system of dams and locks for the canal, and in the sentence that applies to question 9 readers are told that he also recommended suitable homes for workers and sanitation and pest control. The latter does not clearly follow "as a result" of the former, so this expression must be incorrect. In the same way, the latter is not a consequence of the former, so "consequently" is incorrect. The discussion of housing, sanitation, and pest control seem to follow as an addition to the recommendations about the canal, so "on the other hand," which indicates contrast, is also incorrect.

10. A: The sentence is correct as is. No form of punctuation is necessary to break up the phrase "both sanitation and pest control," since the expression "both...and" functions as a single conjunction without the need for punctuation.

11. D: The comma just before the word "each" creates a helpful pause in the sentence that establishes the clarity of meaning. The use of a period or a semicolon creates a fragment where "each of which" begins (since that statement cannot stand on its own as a complete idea). The colon is not clearly necessary, since the information that follows a colon must provide a definition or expansion of the information that comes before it.

12. B: A comma is the best way to set off the statement starting with "that is" in this case. The lack of a comma makes the ideas run together and reduces clarity. The period creates a fragment, and the comma after "that is" but not before it creates confusion in the reading of the sentence.

13. B: This is an example of the comma before a coordinating conjunction. Because the conjunction "and" joins two independent clauses, the comma signals where one ends and the next one begins. The lack of a comma creates a run-on sentence. Additionally, the comma should always fall before the conjunction instead of after it.

14. C: The sentence for question 14 has a series of phrases and clauses embedded in it, and punctuation assists the reader in sorting through these phrases and clauses. The commas set off the most essential information within the paragraph, while the parentheses set off less essential but still useful information. The sole use of commas (as in answer choice A) makes it harder for the reader to recognize the primary and secondary material in the sentence. Brackets are generally used when the writer is offering an aside to the reader – and that is not relevant in this sentence.

38

And the rewording of the sentence (as in answer choice D) actually removes the meaning by making Madison personally responsible for the recommendation, when the sentence actually suggests that the recommendation was part of the Virginia Plan that he drafted.

15. B: Here, it is necessary to choose the most effective opening expression for the sentence. Because the sentence defines or further explains information that has come before, the use of "In other words" is appropriate here. No contrast is indicated, so "On the other hand" and "Nevertheless" are not correct. "Additionally" suggests something more, but it does not encompass the necessary ideas of definition or further explanation.

16. A: The sentence is correct without a change in punctuation or usage. No hyphen or comma is necessary between "small northern" and "large southern," and the comma makes little sense after the state "Delaware" since no pause is necessary or appropriate there.

17. A: Once again, the sentence is correct without a need for change. The comma between "single" and "equal" suggests a pause between a series of modifiers. As a general rule, if you can place "and" between the words, a comma is appropriate: "…each state would be given a single *and* equal voice." "More equal" is never correct: equality either exists or it does not. If two entities are equal, they cannot be more equal. (And if one of them is more equal, then they are not equal at all.) The use of the hyphen is incorrect, because the two words represent separate modifiers instead of a combined modifier.

18. C: The word "state's," with the apostrophe, is the correct expression of a singular possessive noun. No possession exists without the apostrophe, and the apostrophe at the end of the word would suggest possession of plural states – not appropriate to the context of the sentence. The quotation marks also have no place in the context of the sentence.

19. C: "As a result" is the most effective transitional expression in this case, since the information about membership allotment in each house follows as a result of the decisions regarding the Virginia Plan and the New Jersey Plan. "Finally" is not inherently incorrect, but does little to connect the ideas effectively. "Beyond this" and "In consideration" do not work in the context of the sentences.

20. A: This is another instance of the sentence needing no adjustment. The colon creates an indication of definition or further explanation, and the statement about "two representatives and an equal voice for each state" is a further explanation of the statement about equal membership allotment in the Senate. The semicolon and period create fragments, and no punctuation at all makes the ideas run together with little clarity.

21. D: Neither punctuation nor the use of "however" is appropriate in the context. The conjunction "but" creates the necessary sense of contrast, so the addition of "however" is simply repetitive and confusing.

22. B: Answer choice B places a comma after an introductory expression, providing clarity and a hint of a pause for the reader to appreciate the flow of the sentence. The semicolon creates a fragment, since "Under the Articles of Confederation" is not an independent clauses but rather an opening prepositional phrase, and the comma after "the question" makes little sense as no pause is necessary there.

23. C: The period ends one independent clause and allows another to begin. Answer choice A provides a comma splice to join the sentences incorrectly. The word "however" is not a coordinating conjunction, so it cannot join the two independent clauses as a conjunction would. And the word "while" adds little to the meaning contained within the statements.

24. D: The commas on both sides of "though" set off the transitional expression of contrast effectively. A lack of commas makes it difficult for the reader to see the flow of thought within the sentence, and the comma on one side of "though" or the other (but not both) make it difficult to understand what the purpose of the word is between "Philadelphia" and "the delegates."

25. C: The hyphen turns the expression "much-needed" into a single adjective that modifies "balance." The commas serve no purpose, since "much" is not a separate modifier for "balance" but rather modifies "needed." The slash has no place, since "much" and "needed" are not alternative word selections for the sentence.

26. D: Commas are often "road signs" in sentences, telling the reader where to pause and take a breath. In the case of question 26, the sentence needs a comma after an opening phrase to create a slight pause before the main clause of the sentence. The period creates a fragment, and the word "Constitution" refers to the official name of a document, so it should be capitalized.

27. A: A colon is correct and even useful in this case. Colons indicate that whatever follows will define, explain, or expand on the material that came just before. The sentence notes that Adams and Jefferson ran against one another, and the statement that follows explains the parties with which they were affiliated and the differences in their political platforms. The period is not unacceptable, but it is not the most effective form of punctuation. The comma alone creates a comma splice and thus a run-on sentence, and the comma and coordinating conjunction make the sentences read awkwardly.

28. C: The conjunction "and" (with no comma necessary) creates a natural flow of thought between the two statements "had little respect for one another" and "had been running *against* one another." The comma with the word "they" (and no conjunction) creates a run-on sentence, while comma alone without the word "and" reads awkwardly. The semicolon is unnecessary, because the sentence is a single independent clause with two verbs, instead of two independent clauses.

29. B: The comma provides a pause between "system" and "giving" and improves the flow of thought within the sentence. The lack of a comma, while not technically incorrect, makes it more difficult for the reader to decipher the progress of thought in the sentence. The period creates a fragment; the colon is unnecessary for defining, explaining, or expanding in this case.

30. A: The word "President" is always capitalized when it refers to the President of the United States, even when it is not applied as a title next to a name.

31. C: The phrase "as everyone hoped and expected" is an aside on the part of the writer. Because an aside is not a necessary part of the sentence – and the sentence can function without it – the aside can be placed within parentheses. The lack of any punctuation around the expression creates an awkward flow of thought in the sentence. The semicolons create a fragment, and the rewording does little to improve the meaning of the sentence.

32. D: Transitional expression such as "however" need commas around them, on both sides of the expression, to set them off. The lack of punctuation, while not completely incorrect, causes the ideas to run into one another. Commas on one side or the other create confusion about the role the expression plays in the sentence.

33. D: The comma before the word "who" offers a slight pause in the sentence without stopping the flow of thought for the reader. The period and the semicolon create a fragment, and the colon has no place in defining, explaining, or expanding within this sentence.

34. B: A comma belongs before a coordinating conjunction. The word "who" does little to improve the meaning of the sentence and does more to create an awkward reading, and the comma without the conjunction creates a run-on sentence.

35. C: There are several layers of punctuation embedded in this sentence, with the commas around the phrase beginning "led intensely by" and the parentheses around the phrase beginning "who disliked both men." The reader should recognize that the primary phrase explains that the election discussion in the House was led by Hamilton. The mention of his feelings for both men is more of an aside and belongs with parentheses. It is important to remember, though, that the parentheses are part of the larger phrase beginning "led intensely by," to a comma belongs after the parenthetical remark as well.

36. A: The comma is the best way to set off the phrase beginning "the terms of which." The semicolon creates a fragment, while the colon is unnecessary to set off the information that follows. The comma and the coordinating conjunction create an awkward reading of the sentence and do nothing to improve its meaning.

37. B: No comma is necessary before the conjunction "and," because the sentence is a single independent clause with two verbs instead of two independent clauses. The comma without the conjunction "and" creates an awkward flow of thought, while the comma with the addition of the word "he" creates a run-on sentence.

38. A: A dash is the perfect way to offset the expression "in several ways," which is intended to be a quick note at the end of the sentence but requires a more dramatic form of punctuation than merely a comma. The colon is incorrect, because "in several ways" does not define, explain, or expand the material just before it. The period creates a fragment, and the parentheses do not belong, because the use of "in several ways" is a necessary part of the sentence instead of an aside on the part of the author.

39. C: The use of "What is more" to open the sentence indicates that Jefferson had a variety of considerations regarding Louisiana and the purchase of New Orleans. On the one hand, he wanted to ensure that the U.S. could continue using the river and the port. *At the same time*, he wanted to stay out of Europe's problems. There is a sense of slight contrast between the statements that justifies the use of "At the same time." The word "Consequently" suggests an immediate cause-and-effect relationship that is not present within the sentences. "In consideration" also indicates cause and effect. "Incredibly" makes little sense in the context of the sentences.

40. C: The comma in answer choice C sets off the dependent clause and improves the flow of thought within the sentence. The period and the semicolon creates fragments, and the comma with the word "he" (and without the word "although") creates a run-on sentence.

41. D: The addition of the word "because" offers a cause-and-effect scenario that explains Jefferson's unwillingness to consider the full Louisiana Territory. The comma alone is a comma splice and thus creates a run-on sentence. The word "and" offers little to improve the flow of thought, and the word "but" creates contrast where the context does not call for it.

42. B: Again, no comma is necessary, because the conjunction joins two verbs instead of two independent clauses. The comma alone creates a sense of items in a series, but there are only two in

41

the phrase that begins "giving," so no commas are necessary between them. The word "yet" makes little sense and adds nothing to improve the meaning of the sentence.

43. C: No apostrophe or other punctuation is necessary here: "the states currently held" is accurate on its own. The singular "state," while not technically incorrect, is not accurate within the context, because there was more than one state within the United States in 1802.

44. A: The sentence is correct with no added punctuation, because the conjunction "but" is not a coordinating conjunction. The semicolon and the period are unnecessary, since the conjunction joins two verbs within a single independent clause. The addition of "they" creates two independent clauses, but answer choice D is incorrect, because there is now no coordinating conjunction to accompany it.

45. A: Once again, the sentence is correct as it is. The commas on both sides of "the most Constitutional of Presidents" set off the expression and improve the flow of thought within the sentence. The lack of commas causes the ideas to run into each other awkwardly, while the single comma after "Presidents" makes it difficult to decipher the role of the phrase within the sentence. The colon has no place and actually creates a fragment.

46. D: The phrase "In other words" signals that the writer will be restating a previous comment to ensure that its meaning is clear to the reader. In the first sentence, the writer notes that "the actual amount of land was not entirely known" after the purchase of the Louisiana Territory. The writer follows this up by clarifying that neither the United States nor France knew exactly how much land it was, so the expression "In other words" makes sense at the start of the second sentence. "On the other hand" suggests contrast that is not present in the context of the sentence. "At the same time" hints at contrast, while "What is more" indicates an addition that makes the second sentence seem repetitive instead of clarifying.

47. C: Answer choice C correctly separates the two independent clauses with a semicolon. The comma represents a comma splice and creates a run-on sentence. The conjunction "but" is repetitive since it is used earlier in the sentence, and the conjunction "yet" makes no sense in the context of the statement – no contrast is indicated between the mention of unclaimed territory and the comment about Jefferson sending the Corps of Discovery to the shores of the Pacific.

48. A: The comma offsets the appositive phrase by creating a slight pause but without disjointing the meaning of the sentence. The lack of a comma makes the ideas run together awkwardly. The dash should usually indicate a sense of drama or significance in the information that follows, but the note about Captain Lewis being an Army captain and friend of President Jefferson is hardly dramatic or surprising. The period with the use of "Who" creates a fragment.

49. A: Answer choice A reflects a somewhat obscure punctuation rule, so the use of the commas after both city and state are, in fact, correct. With correct punctuation usage, a comma belongs after the city as well as the state if the sentence continues after the mention of the state. The parentheses would only be necessary if the writer were clarifying which Pittsburgh is under discussion. Since there is only one and mention of both city and state fit into the context of the paragraphs (with the writer mentioning other cities and states in the paragraph), the name of the state does not need to go in parentheses.

50. D: The comma prevents the expression "their journey complete" from becoming a fragment. The period and the semicolon create fragments, because the expression cannot stand on its own as a complete sentence. The lack of a comma hinders the progress of thought by making the ideas run into each other awkwardly. What is more, as noted in the answer for question 49, a comma belongs

42

after both city and state when the sentence continues after the mention of the state, so the lack of a comma after "Missouri" is incorrect.

51. B: The possessive form of the plural "women" is "women's," with the apostrophe and the letter "s" at the end of the word. The word requires an "s" to be possessive, so answer choices A and D are incorrect. The context calls for the word to be plural, so "woman's" (answer choice C) is also incorrect.

52. D: The comma before the word "where" signals the start of a dependent clause and provides a slight pause in the flow of thought. The period and the semicolon create fragments. The colon is unnecessary, because the material that follows does not define, explain, or expand on what came before.

53. C: Commas must be present on both sides of the expression or not at all, since the name "Colonel William H. Bright" represents a nonessential appositive. The dashes are unnecessary, because the appositive does not require an element of dramatic pause that dashes tend to provide.

54. A: For correct usage, hyphens must be present before "year" and "old," because the combination of the three words represents a single adjective. One hyphen, before either "year" or "old," or no hyphens at all, does not accurately create the adjective.

55. D: No punctuation is necessary before the conjunction because it joins two verbs that go with a single subject, instead of two independent clauses. What is more, the semicolon creates a fragment, and the comma without the conjunction does nothing to improve the flow of thought within the sentence and actually makes it read a little more awkwardly.

56. C: The word "East" should be capitalized when it refers to a region of the United States (just as the other regions are capitalized: the North, the South, and the West). The colon is unnecessary in the context of the sentence, and the comma after "in" makes no sense, because "in the East" is a simple prepositional phrase.

57. B: A question mark belongs at the end of an interrogative sentence. The other answer choices incorrectly present the statement as a declaration instead of a question, so they cannot be correct.

58. B: Question 58 poses a basic declarative statement that needs to internal punctuation. The comma after "But" is unnecessary, because it is not followed by a nonessential expression that requires a comma later in the sentence. The semicolon creates a fragment. The exclamation point could technically work, but the internal comma after "But" makes answer choice D incorrect.

59. A: The dash offers a slight dramatic pause and is correct in the context of the sentence. The colon, while not necessarily incorrect in the context, is not as effective as the dash. The semicolon turns the phrase "a jury composed entirely of men" into a fragment. The rewording of the sentence (in answer choice D) removes the necessary sense of drama that the phrase "a jury composed entirely of men" provides.

60. C: The statement "when Congress passed the 19th Amendment" is a dependent clause that requires a comma to create a slight pause in the flow of thought, while the conjunction "and" that follows creates a new independent clause. The colon has no place in the context of the sentence, and the apostrophe after "States" is entirely incorrect here. The comma without the conjunction "and" represents a comma splice.

61. D: The phrase "The most notorious" indicates a singular subject, so the expression needs the singular verb "was." The plural verb incorrectly makes "accidents" (within the prepositional phrase) the subject. The verbs "would have been" and "would be" make little sense in the context of the sentence.

62. B: No internal punctuation is necessary in the statement "Triangle Shirtwaist Factory fire occurring in March of 1911." The use of "that was occurring" is awkward in the context of the sentence, and the comma after "March" is unnecessary, because the preposition of indicates the connection to the year.

63. D: Again, no internal punctuation is unnecessary, because the phrase "horrified and outraged" indicate a plural verb for the subject "fire." Answer choice B rewords the sentence to little purpose, and answer choice C capitalizes "Society" when it does not clearly require capitalization in the context of the sentence.

64. B: The word "its" as a possessive pronoun needs no punctuation. Any apostrophe in the word makes it incorrect, and the apostrophe in "it's" creates the contraction for "it is."

65. C: The comma before "except" offers a slight pause in the sentence and improves or clarifies the flow of thought. The colon does not belong anywhere in the statement, and the period before "Except" creates a fragment.

66. A: Perhaps surprisingly, the word "sneaked" is correct usage. "Sneaking," in this case, does not work due to the past tense context of the sentence, and any form of "snuck" is incorrect as the past tense for "sneak."

67. D: The phrase "As a result" creates a natural transitional expression to show the cause-and-effect relationship between the owners leaving when the fire was discovered and the workers being unable to get out. The other transitional expressions ("Likewise," "Not surprisingly," and "However") do little to improve the meaning of the sentence, and the phrase "Not surprisingly" adds an editorial comment about the behavior of the owners that is not appropriate to a historical description (nor does it follow naturally from the author's tone earlier in the excerpt).

68. C: The addition of "while" avoids the comma splice and run-on sentence that the original statement creates. The conjunction requires a comma in this case, because it is a coordinating conjunction that joins two independent clauses. The use of "still" also creates a run-on, because it creates a second independent clause instead of a dependent clause (as "while" does).

69. A: The sentence is correct in its original form. The material that follows the colon explains the specific safety flaws that created the tragic event. The semicolon and the period create fragments with the list of information that follows. The comma and the conjunction "and" do little to improve the meaning of the sentence and ultimately create an awkwardly worded sentence.

70. B: The comma before "such as" is appropriate to indicate a pause before the introduction of the material that follows. The colon would work without the phrase "such as," but it does not work along with that phrase. The semicolon and the period create fragments.

Practice Test #2

Job Knowledge

1. The social scientists most likely to study the role of kinship relationships within a cultural group are:

    a. economists.
    b. political scientists.
    c. psychologists.
    d. anthropologists

2. Which of these was NOT an immediate consequence of the Age of Exploration?

    a. the development of more accurate navigation instruments
    b. the introduction of new foods and other goods to Europe
    c. the decline of England as a world power
    d. the discovery of new lands where people might seek a better life

3. Which of these countries does NOT share a border with Israel?

    a. Jordan
    b. Saudi Arabia
    c. Lebanon
    d. Egypt

4. Which of these statements about Africa is true?

    a. It is nearly twice the size of the continental United States.
    b. It includes about 20 percent of the world's land surface but only 12 percent of its population.
    c. Almost the entire continent lies south of the equator.
    d. Nearly 50 percent of southern Africa consists of rain forest.

5. Which of these presidents most greatly expanded the power of the presidency?

    a. Thomas Jefferson
    b. Herbert Hoover
    c. Lyndon Johnson
    d. George W. Bush

6. The physical geography of a region most directly affects:

    a. the religious beliefs of the native population.
    b. the family structure of the native population.
    c. the dietary preferences of the native population.
    d. the language spoken by the native population.

7. Most of the region known in ancient times as Mesopotamia is located in the present-day nation of:

    a. Iran.
    b. Saudi Arabia.
    c. Turkmenistan.
    d. Iraq.

8. A nation that is NOT a member of NAFTA is:

    a. Mexico.
    b. Brazil.
    c. the United States.
    d. Canada.

9. One reason for Jefferson's opposition to the Bank of the United States was that he:

    a. did not think the Bank would effectively further his goal of establishing a strong central government.
    b. was a strict constructionist.
    c. believed the Bank would give an unfair advantage to the southern states.
    d. distrusted the fiscal policies of the Democratic-Republicans.

10. The main reason that the Federal Reserve Board lowers interest rates is to:

    a. lower prices.
    b. stimulate consumer spending.
    c. encourage international trade.
    d. control inflation.

11. The reforms set in motion by the Russian leader Mikhail Gorbachev played an important role in:

    a. the breakup of the Soviet Union.
    b. creating economic prosperity in post-Cold War Russia.
    c. prolonging the Cold War.
    d. ending the war in Bosnia.

12. Which of the following best describes the significance of the U.S. Supreme Court's decision in the Dred Scott case?

    a. The ruling effectively declared slavery to be a violation of the Constitution.
    b. The ruling guaranteed full citizenship rights to freed slaves.
    c. The ruling turned many Southerners against the Supreme Court.
    d. The ruling furthered the gap between North and South and hastened the Civil War.

13. Which of these states was NOT one of the original 13 colonies?

    a. Maine
    b. Rhode Island
    c. New Hampshire
    d. New Jersey

14. Article I of the United States Constitution includes the following paragraph:

   No title of nobility shall be granted by the United States: and no person holding any office of profit or trust under them, shall, without the consent of the Congress, accept of any present, emolument, office, or title, of any kind whatever, from any king, prince, or foreign state.

This paragraph most directly reflects the influence of:

    a. John Locke.
    b. Baron de Montesquieu.
    c. Jean-Jacques Rousseau.
    d. Thomas Paine.

15. Under the Articles of Confederation, Congress was not granted the power to:
    a. wage war and make treaties.
    b. regulate Indian affairs.
    c. appoint military officers.
    d. levy taxes.

16. Which of the following accurately describes the process by which government officials may be impeached and removed from office?
    a. Charges are brought by the House of Representatives and tried in the Senate.
    b. Charges are brought by the Senate and tried in the House of Representatives.
    c. Charges are brought by the Attorney-General and tried in Congress.
    d. Charges are brought by both houses of Congress and tried in the Supreme Court.

17. According to Karl Marx, two groups that are in continual conflict are:
    a. farmers and landowners.
    b. workers and owners.
    c. kings and nobles.
    d. politicians and voters.

18. The power of the President to veto an act of Congress is an example of:
    a. checks and balances.
    b. separation of powers.
    c. judicial review.
    d. advice and consent.

19. Congress can override the Presidential veto of a bill by:
    a. a majority vote in the House and a two-thirds majority in the Senate.
    b. a two-thirds vote in the House and a majority in the Senate.
    c. a majority vote in both the House and the Senate.
    d. a two-thirds vote in both the House and the Senate.

20. The main author of the Bill of Rights was:
    a. George Washington.
    b. John Adams.
    c. Thomas Jefferson.
    d. James Madison.

21. Which of the following is NOT an example of a shared, or concurrent, power?
    a. the power to build roads
    b. the power to coin money
    c. the power to collect taxes
    d. the power to establish courts

22. The social science that focuses primarily on how a society produces and distributes goods is:
    a. sociology.
    b. anthropology.
    c. psychology.
    d. economics.

23. When state legislatures pass laws that regulate driving, marriage, and public education, they are exercising their:

    a. implied, or suggested, powers.
    b. shared, or concurrent, powers.
    c. expressed, or enumerated, powers.
    d. reserved powers.

24. The main purpose of the census is to:

    a. monitor illegal immigration.
    b. apportion seats in the House of Representatives.
    c. help determine federal income tax rates.
    d. reapportion seats in the United States Senate.

25. The First Amendment to the Constitution deals mainly with:

    a. the right of free expression.
    b. the right to a speedy and public trial.
    c. protection from cruel and unusual punishment.
    d. freedom from unreasonable search and seizure.

26. The Federal Deposit Insurance Corporation (FDIC) and the Securities and Exchange Commission (SEC) were created during the presidency of:

    a. Theodore Roosevelt.
    b. Woodrow Wilson.
    c. Franklin Roosevelt.
    d. Harry Truman.

27. The leading producers of petroleum in Latin America are:

    a. Argentina and Bolivia.
    b. Brazil and Guatemala.
    c. Mexico and Venezuela.
    d. Columbia and Uruguay.

28. Under the United States Constitution, the power to tax and borrow is:

    a. implied.
    b. shared.
    c. expressed.
    d. reserved.

29. Which of the following is NOT a contingency for organizing?

    a. Size
    b. Strategy
    c. Technology
    d. Leadership

30. Which of the following pieces of legislation guarantees equal pay for men and women doing equal work?

    a. Fair Labor Standards Act of 1938
    b. Equal Pay Act of 1963
    c. Civil Rights Act of 1964
    d. Occupational Safety and Health Act of 1970

31. Which of the following is NOT a source of power that leaders may exercise?

    a. Legitimate
    b. Illegitimate
    c. Coercive
    d. Expert

32. Which of the following is the average percentage of work time managers spend dealing with conflict?

    a. 5%
    b. 10%
    c. 15%
    d. 20%

33. Which of the following is a condition that can lead to conflict?

    a. Role ambiguities
    b. Scarce resources
    c. Task interdependencies
    d. All of the above

34. Which form of communication is the "richest"?

    a. Email
    b. Telephone
    c. Face-to-face
    d. Handwritten note

35. Which of the following terms describes communication between individuals in different units and at different levels in a company?

    a. Vertical
    b. Horizontal
    c. Top-down
    d. Diagonal

36. Which of the following is NOT an advantage of group decision-making?

    a. Additional informational resources
    b. Different decision styles
    c. Greater understanding of underlying issue
    d. Additional information to weigh

37. Which of the following is the BEST definition for the term *human capital*?

    a. The economic value of the skills and abilities of a company's workforce
    b. The economic value of the combined salaries of a company's workforce
    c. The economic value of the combined bonuses of a company's workforce
    d. The economic cost a company would accrue to replace its workforce

38. What is the name for lawsuits filed against employers who have not carefully reviewed a job applicant's background?

    a. Negligent hiring suits
    b. Careless hiring suits
    c. Wrongful hiring suits
    d. Tortious hiring suits

39. A steak dinner at a restaurant costs $15.99. If a man buys a steak dinner for himself and 4 friends, what will the total cost be?

    a. $63.96
    b. $68.45
    c. $74.76
    d. $79.95

40. A woman has two bank accounts. One contains $329 and awards 4% in interest each month. The other contains $921 and awards 7% in interest each month. What will the combined value of her two accounts be at the end of the month?

    a. $342.08
    b. $985.47
    c. $1250.00
    d. $1327.63

41. A grocery manager sells 2 bags of potatoes for each bag of carrots. He also sells 6 bags of onions for each bag of potatoes. If he sells 12 bags of onions, how many bags of carrots will he sell?

    a. 1
    b. 2
    c. 3
    d. 4

42. A man invested $150 in the stock market. During the first week, he lost $45. During the second week, he tripled his money. How much does he have at the end of the second week?

    a. $105
    b. $210
    c. $315
    d. $420

43. A woman earns $65,000 each year. She must pay 36% of this amount ($65,000) in income tax. How much income tax does the woman pay each year?

    a. $14,300
    b. $23,400
    c. $32,800
    d. $41,600

44. A classroom has 15 boys and 13 girls. If 10 more girls join the class, what is the ratio of girls to boys?
    a. 15 : 23
    b. 13 : 15
    c. 10 : 15
    d. 23 : 15

45. A man works three jobs. In one week, he earns $500 at one, $65 at the second, and $175 at the third. What is his total weekly salary?
    a. $240
    b. $565
    c. $675
    d. $740

46. Which statement best describes the role of natural selection in Charles Darwin's theory of evolution?
    a. Natural selection describes the diversity of environmental pressures.
    b. Natural selection is the process by which individual organisms adapt.
    c. Natural selection explains how organisms inherit acquired characteristics.
    d. Natural selection is the mechanism by which species are said to evolve.

47. How did Russia's participation in World War I influence the Russian Revolution?
    a. Civilian suffering and military setbacks served as a catalyst for revolutionary forces.
    b. Nicholas III capitalized on battlefield successes to temporarily silence critics.
    c. The government eased laws banning collective action by factory workers to appease social discontent about the war.
    d. Anti-government protesters temporarily ceased protesting to show patriotism in a difficult war

48. Which statement best describes how the Spanish-American War in 1898 shaped the international standing of the United States?
    a. The United States gained new international respect through the strategic brilliance and efficiency of the U.S. Army.
    b. The U.S. weakened its moral authority by being the first nation in the conflict to declare war.
    c. The sinking of the U.S. Battleship Maine cast international doubts on the power of the U.S. Navy.
    d. The United States gained new international power by acquiring Guam, Puerto Rico, and the Philippines.

49. During the Cuban Missile Crisis, what did Soviet President Nikita Khrushchev demand in exchange for the removal of Soviet missile launching sites from Cuba?
    a. A guarantee that the United States would not invade Cuba
    b. The removal of U.S. missile launching sites from an island off the Soviet coast
    c. An apology for the U.S. naval blockade that prevented Soviet access to Cuba
    d. Negotiations regarding the production of nuclear weapons

50. How did isolationism most influence American society in the decade following World War I?

a. It shaped a temporarily strong economy as the U.S. avoided the troubled economies of postwar Europe.

b. It led to a system of admitting immigrants according to quotas based on their national origins.

c. It guided the U.S. government's decision to strengthen its navy as a safeguard against foreign attacks.

d. It influenced the collapse of trade deals, allowing U.S. companies access to oil in Colombia and in Middle Eastern countries.

51. Which statement best describes how the 1944 passage of the G.I. Bill most influenced U.S. society?

a. It dramatically increased retention in the U.S. military.

b. It offered limited free housing for veterans.

c. It helped create a new middle class in U.S. society.

d. It transformed the work force by privileging veterans.

52. Mecca is an important site for Muslims primarily because:

a. it is the birthplace of the prophet Muhammad.

b. according to the Koran, the Second Coming will occur in Mecca.

c. Muhammad fled to Mecca from Medina in 622 A.D,

d. it is home of the Ka'ba, a holy structure said to be built by Abraham.

53. What is the Noble Eightfold Path in Buddhism?

a. Samsara, the cycle of birth, death, and rebirth

b. Moral life as a means to end suffering

c. The Buddhist precepts of ethical conduct

d. The realization that self is an illusion

54. Which of the following statements best describes how Cubism reflected a changing world in the early 20th century?

a. It depicted subjects from multiple perspectives.

b. It portrayed the human body as sacrosanct.

c. It eschewed rationality in favor of emotion.

d. It used unusually vivid colors and color schemes.

55. World population growth has most significantly impacted which of the following aspects of Earth's physical environment?

a. Deforestation

b. Increased biodiversity

c. Shrinking ocean "dead zones"

d. Mass extinction events

56. In 1973, the U.S. Congress passed the War Powers Act. How did the Act reassert congressional authority relative to that of the President?

a. It mandated congressional approval for funding war-related expenses.
b. It required the President to submit regular reports to Congress regarding conflicts lasting more than 60 days.
c. It restricted the power of the President to suspend key elements of the Constitution.
d. It limited the length of time the President could dispatch combat troops without congressional approval.

57. The U.S. government is best understood as a federalist government because:

a. the legislative branch consists of two representative bodies.
b. it is a representative democracy rather than a direct democracy.
c. political power is divided between the federal government and the states.
d. a national Constitution shapes national legislation.

58. Civic responsibility differs from personal responsibility in that the subject matter of civic responsibility is mainly:

a. fair reporting of government actions.
b. fair dealings between governments.
c. a person's responsibilities as a citizen.
d. a person's responsibilities as a government worker.

59. In the United States, the Electoral College elects the President and Vice President. The number of Electoral College members allowed to each state is equal to:

a. the state's number of U.S. Representatives plus counties.
b. the state's number of U.S. Senators plus Representatives.
c. the state's number of U.S. Representatives plus state Secretaries.
d. the state's number of U.S. Senators plus counties.

60. How does the executive branch of a parliamentary democracy differ from that in the United States' form of government?

a. It appoints the legislative branch.
b. It is a committee of the judicial branch.
c. It is appointed by the judicial branch.
d. It is a committee of the legislative branch.

English Expression

DIRECTIONS: In the passages that follow, words and phrases are underlined and numbered. Read the alternate suggestions for each underlined part and choose the one that seems to work best with the style and tone of the article and is grammatically correct. The original response is always listed as the first option. Read each passage through before reviewing the questions and responses.

Questions 1-10 pertain to the following excerpt of four paragraphs:

The era known as the First Great Awakening is generally believed to have begun in the American colonies around 1740. Massachusetts pastor Jonathan Edwards preached a (1) <u>now-famous</u> sermon that rocked his congregation to its core and initiated a revival in the colonies. This sermon, (2) <u>Sinners in the Hands of an Angry God</u>, impressed on his listeners the need to take the state of their souls seriously. (3) <u>Edwards arguing from a Puritan and thus Calvinist background believed</u> that mankind's fate was entirely in the hands of God and that God had the authority to condemn sinners to hell at any time. It was only as a result of God's mercy and grace that sinners were saved through repentance.

Edwards may have prompted the first flames of a revival in the colonies, but it was the enthusiastic English preacher (4) <u>George Whitefield who fanned the flames</u> and spread the fire of a religious awakening throughout the colonies. Whitefield traveled through the colonies, preaching to large crowds of more than 10,000 in open fields. Other preachers tried to follow (5) <u>Whitefields</u> lead and style of delivering his salvation message, but none became as famous or as popular as Whitefield.

This period of revival, described later as the First Great Awakening, had arguable (6) <u>affects</u> on the colonists beyond the purely spiritual. Benjamin Franklin first heard Whitefield preach in (7) <u>Philadelphia, and was impressed by Whitefield's magnetism</u>, as well as his vocal range. Whitefield failed to convert the Deist Franklin, but Franklin viewed Whitefield as a valuable part of encouraging democracy within the colonies. Whitefield reached out to every sinner alike, regardless of class, gender, or even race. (8) <u>Whitefield was one of the first to preach to the slaves within the colonies.</u> By teaching that all are equal in the eyes of God, Whitefield prompted a mood of egalitarianism among American colonists.

Historians continue to disagree about the role that the First Great Awakening played in the American Revolution. Some see the event primarily (9) <u>in religious terms; arguing that a religious revival</u> could only extend so far into American politics. (10) <u>Others however view the event</u> as an important step along the path toward revolution. The Awakening diminished the authority of the Anglican Church within the colonies, thus reducing one connection to England, and the uniqueness of the Awakening for Americans encouraged a mood of nationalism to sweep the colonies. While the long-term impact will always be a subject for debate, historians do agree that the Awakening represents an important element in shaping moral views in America and encouraging the attitude of individualism that would come to define the 19th century in America.

1.

    a. now-famous
    b. now famous
    c. nowfamous
    d. now/famous

2.

    a. Sinners in the Hands of an Angry God
    b. 'Sinners in the Hands of an Angry God'
    c. "Sinners in the Hands of an Angry God"
    d. Sinners, in the Hands of an Angry God

3.

    a. Edwards arguing from a Puritan and thus Calvinist background believed
    b. Edwards, arguing from a Puritan and thus Calvinist background, believed
    c. Edwards, arguing from a Puritan and thus Calvinist background believed
    d. Edwards arguing from a Puritan, and thus Calvinist, background believed

4.

    a. George Whitefield who fanned the flames
    b. George Whitefield: who fanned the flames
    c. George Whitefield; who fanned the flames
    d. George Whitefield, who fanned the flames

5.

    a. Whitefields
    b. Whitefield's
    c. Whitefields'
    d. Whitefield's'

6.

    a. affects
    b. affecting
    c. effects
    d. effecting

7.

    a. Philadelphia, and was impressed by Whitefield's magnetism
    b. Philadelphia, was impressed by Whitefield's magnetism
    c. Philadelphia and was impressed by Whitefield's magnetism
    d. Philadelphia; and was impressed by Whitefield's magnetism

8.

    a. Whitefield was one of the first to preach to the slaves within the colonies.
    b. (Whitefield was one of the first to preach to the slaves within the colonies.)
    c. [Whitefield was one of the first to preach to the slaves within the colonies.]
    d. Whitefield was one of the first to preach to the slaves within the colonies!

9.
   a. in religious terms; arguing that a religious revival
   b. in religious terms. Arguing that a religious revival
   c. in religious terms – arguing that a religious revival
   d. in religious terms, arguing that a religious revival

10.
   a. Others however view the event
   b. Others, however view the event
   c. Others, however, view the event
   d. Others however: view the event

Questions 11-25 pertain to the following excerpt of five paragraphs:

The First Great Awakening arguably influenced the immediate political situation in the United States. The Second Great Awakening, on the other hand, had a decided effect (11) <u>on the moral, and social development</u> among the American people. What is more, the Second Great Awakening did more to fracture Christian denominations, while the First Great Awakening united most Americans under (12) <u>a single-sense of spiritual purpose</u>. The Second Great Awakening saw the rise of (13) <u>Adventist teaching and Restoration theology: as well as the development of the Church of Jesus Christ of Latter-day Saints</u>.

The revivals of the Second Great Awakening began in upstate New York, where a series of religious experiences influenced the region. One of the early movements was that of Adventism, which intended to prepare believers for (14) <u>the Second Coming of Jesus Christ (the Second Advent)</u>. Adventism taught that Christ would be returning soon, so believers should prepare their souls and get ready for heaven. While Adventism viewed itself as a new and separate denomination, the Adventist preachers saw a strong response from (15) <u>the established Baptist and Methodist denominations, as well</u>.

The Restoration Movement also sought to prepare believers (16) <u>for the Second Coming, but the approach was significantly different</u> than that of the Adventists. The Restoration preachers encouraged believers to return to a form of Christianity that could be deemed more (17) <u>"pure"</u>. They did this by stripping away all religious ornaments of the (18) <u>high churches; such as the Anglican or Episcopal Church;</u> and practicing Christianity in a way that would reflect the early church as closely as possible. The Restoration Movement saw the return of Christ (19) <u>as imminent. Believers should live</u> as closely to the original teachings and practices as possible.

(20) <u>The Church of Jesus Christ of Latter-day Saints also known as the Mormon Church, grew out of the Restoration movement</u> but developed into a unique organization. The theological positions that developed among the Mormon believers are widely rejected (21) <u>among the Christian Church: which to this day does not recognize</u> the Mormon Church as a part of traditional Christianity. As a result of the conflicts that they faced, the Mormon believers relocated en masse (22) <u>from the Midwest to Utah. Where they established</u> a distinctly Mormon territory.

The immediate influences of the Second Great Awakening applied primarily to the moral attitudes among Americans as they moved out West. Over the long term,

56

however, political changes resulted from the religious revivals of the Second Great Awakening. Some of the most significant political movements were Abolition in the mid-19th century and Prohibition and (23) women's suffrage in the early 20th century. The awakening resulted in a push for such elements as pure living (hence the need for a life without alcohol) and individual (24) freedom for all, explaining the need for the abolition of slavery and women's right to vote. (25) Even in modern American politics, the Second Great Awakening continues to be felt, with the large numbers of voters that are part of denominations deriving from this religious period.

11.

    a. on the moral, and social development
    b. on the moral but social development
    c. on the moral and social development
    d. on the moral, social development

12.

    a. a single-sense of spiritual purpose
    b. a single sense of spiritual purpose
    c. a single/sense of spiritual-purpose
    d. a single, sense of spiritual purpose

13.

    a. Adventist teaching and Restoration theology: as well as the development of the Church of Jesus Christ of Latter-day Saints
    b. Adventist teaching and Restoration theology as well as the development of the Church of Jesus Christ of Latter-day Saints
    c. Adventist teaching and Restoration theology; as well as the development of the Church of Jesus Christ of Latter-day Saints
    d. Adventist teaching and Restoration theology, as well as the development of the Church of Jesus Christ of Latter-day Saints

14.

    a. the Second Coming of Jesus Christ (the Second Advent)
    b. the Second Coming of Jesus Christ, the Second Advent
    c. the Second Coming of Jesus Christ [the Second Advent]
    d. the Second Coming of Jesus Christ – the Second Advent –

15.

    a. the established Baptist and Methodist denominations, as well
    b. the established Baptist and Methodist denominations; as well
    c. the established Baptist and Methodist denominations. As well
    d. the established Baptist and Methodist denominations as well

16.

    a. for the Second Coming, but the approach was significantly different
    b. for the Second Coming but the approach was significantly different
    c. for the Second Coming; but the approach was significantly different
    d. for the Second Coming. But the approach was significantly different

17.

 a. "pure".
 b. "pure"!
 c. "pure."
 d. 'pure'.

18.

 a. high churches; such as the Anglican or Episcopal Church;
 b. high churches (such as the Anglican or Episcopal Church)
 c. high churches such as the Anglican or Episcopal Church
 d. high churches: such as the Anglican or Episcopal Church:

19.

 a. as imminent. Believers should live
 b. as imminent, so believers should live
 c. as imminent so, believers should live
 d. as imminent, believers should live

20.

 a. The Church of Jesus Christ of Latter-day Saints also known as the Mormon Church grew out of the Restoration movement
 b. The Church of Jesus Christ of Latter-day Saints, also known as the Mormon Church grew out of the Restoration movement
 c. The Church of Jesus Christ of Latter-day Saints also known as the Mormon Church grew out of the Restoration movement
 d. The Church of Jesus Christ of Latter-day Saints, also known as the Mormon Church, grew out of the Restoration movement

21.

 a. among the Christian Church: which to this day does not recognize
 b. among the Christian Church; which to this day does not recognize
 c. among the Christian Church, which to this day does not recognize
 d. among the Christian Church, which, to this day does not recognize

22.

 a. from the Midwest to Utah. Where they established
 b. from the Midwest to Utah, where they established
 c. from the Midwest to Utah – where they established
 d. from the Midwest to Utah, and they established

23.

 a. women's suffrage
 b. Women's suffrage
 c. women's Suffrage
 d. Women's Suffrage

24.

a. freedom for all, explaining the need
b. freedom for all: explaining the need
c. freedom for all. This explains the need
d. freedom for all (explaining the need

25.

a. Even in modern American politics, the Second Great Awakening
b. Even in modern American politics the Second Great Awakening
c. Even in modern American politics; the Second Great Awakening
d. Even in modern American politics. The Second Great Awakening

Questions 26-37 pertain to the following excerpt of four paragraphs:

The American Revolution was the result of events that occurred (26) <u>over a number of years; with the colonists resisting</u> what they viewed as imposition from the British government. One of the imposing changes that the (27) <u>colonists'</u> resisted most strenuously was the Stamp Act of 1765. This act resulted in a tax on printed material – a tax that enraged the colonists. The tax was not necessarily levied without cause. From 1756 to 1763, the British fought the Seven Years' War, known as the French and Indian War to the colonists. Following the war, the British established troops in the colonies to provide ongoing defense. As a result, the British believed that the colonists needed to contribute (28) <u>to supporting the troops, because the troops were there</u>, in part at least, for their own protection.

Taxes were not new in the colonies, but this tax proved to be particularly onerous to the colonists. For one, the tax was levied entirely at the discretion of the British government. (29) <u>On the other hand</u>, an act was passed in England, and the colonists became responsible for paying a tax. In the larger scheme of things, however, the tax revealed an increasingly frustrating issue (30) <u>for the colonists, they had no representation in Parliament</u>. In England, the citizens voted for local representatives who functioned as their voice in Parliament. (31) <u>The colonists had no such representation they were taxed without having any say in the decision.</u>

(32) <u>Upon hearing the news of the Stamp Act, a quick and angry response was made by the colonists</u>. They created the Stamp Act Congress in New York, which sent a formal petition to Parliament in objection to the new tax. They resisted paying the tax to the newly created stamp tax collectors and even resorted to violent protests against the tax collectors (most of who resigned to avoid personal danger). (33) <u>It was not only the colonists, but also the merchants</u> in Britain who objected to the tax. The stamp tax would place a financial burden on the colonists and result in fewer imports to the colonies from Britain. (34) <u>This, in turn would reduce</u> income in Britain for merchants. The merchants sent a petition of their own to ask Parliament to cancel the tax.

Ultimately, the stamp tax was not collected in the colonies. The strenuous objections (35) <u>from colonists, and merchants</u> succeeded in ending the legislation, and Parliament rescinded the Stamp Act shortly after imposing it. In doing so, Parliament also noted that it retained the right to tax the colonies without official (36) <u>colonial representation</u>. The denial of what they viewed as their rights under

59

English law (37) <u>angered many colonists and the larger result</u> of the failed Stamp Act was the growing chasm in national unity between the colonies and Great Britain.

26.

a. over a number of years; with the colonists resisting
b. over a number of years. With the colonists resisting
c. over a number of years – with the colonists resisting
d. over a number of years, with the colonists resisting

27.

a. colonists'
b. colonists
c. colonist's
d. colonists's

28.

a. to supporting the troops, because the troops were there
b. to supporting the troops because the troops were there
c. to supporting the troops. Because the troops were there
d. to supporting the troops because, the troops were there

29.

a. On the other hand
b. For example
c. In other words
d. Additionally

30.

a. for the colonists they had no representation in Parliament
b. for the colonists: they had no representation in Parliament
c. for the colonists. They had no representation in Parliament
d. for the colonists, but they had no representation in Parliament

31.

a. The colonists had no such representation they were taxed without having any say in the decision.
b. The colonists had no such representation, they were taxed without having any say in the decision.
c. The colonists had no such representation, so they were taxed without having any say in the decision.
d. The colonists had no such representation, but they were taxed without having any say in the decision.

32.

a. Upon hearing the news of the Stamp Act, a quick and angry response was made by the colonists.
b. Upon hearing the news of the Stamp Act a quick and angry response was made by the colonists
c. Upon hearing the news of the Stamp Act, the colonists responded quickly and angrily.
d. Upon hearing the news of the Stamp Act: the colonists responded quickly and angrily.

33.

    a. It was not only the colonists, but also the merchants

    b. It was the colonists not only but the merchants also

    c. It was not only the colonists but also the merchants

    d. It was the colonists and the merchants

34.

    a. This, in turn would reduce

    b. This, in turn, would reduce

    c. This – in turn – would reduce

    d. This in turn would reduce

35.

    a. from colonists, and merchants

    b. from colonists, or merchants

    c. from colonists or merchants

    d. from colonists and merchants

36.

    a. colonial representation

    b. colonial-representation

    c. Colonial Representation

    d. colonial Representation

37.

    a. angered many colonists and the larger result

    b. angered many colonists, and the larger result

    c. angered many colonists, the larger result

    d. angered many colonists. And the larger result

Questions 38-50 pertain to the following excerpt of four paragraphs:

Historians tend to agree that the assassination of Austro-Hungarian Archduke Franz Ferdinand in (38) <u>June of 1914</u> prompted the start of the First World War. The nobleman, who was also the heir presumptive to the Austro-Hungarian throne, was visiting the city of Sarajevo in the empire's province Bosnia Herzegovina. The visit did not come without a measure of animosity on all sides. Austria-Hungary had annexed (39) <u>Bosnia Herzegovina in 1909 a move that angered the nearby Kingdom of Serbia</u> due to the large number of Slavic Serbs who lived in Bosnia Herzegovina. As the archduke was touring the city, a gunman fired at him and his wife, killing both within minutes. The assassin proved to be a Serbian member of the Black Hand, which was an organization dedicated to resisting the Austro-Hungarian absorption of the Slavic peoples into (40) <u>it's</u> empire.

What might have been (41) <u>an isolated, albeit tragic, event in history, ultimately set in motion</u> a chain of events that led to multiple nations declaring war on one another. Three weeks after the assassination, the Austro-Hungarian Emperor Franz Josef (42) <u>demanded retribution from Serbia; and even accused the Serbian government</u> of being involved with Black Hand activities. The emperor's official mandate required justice for the crime, with the promise that Austria-Hungary would strip Serbia of its sovereignty (43) <u>if justice were denied</u>. Historians now believe that Austria-Hungary had no intention for Serbia to agree, given the offensive demands that were made. Instead, the powerful empire expected the Serbian government to decline, thus justifying the (44) <u>empires' war</u> on Serbia. A successful war on Serbia would bring even more Balkan territories into the empire.

Serbia was not without resources, however. As a Slavic nation, Serbia was close to Russia, and a war with Russia was not part of Austria-Hungary's plan. To protect itself, the Austro-Hungarian government turned to its (45) <u>long time</u> ally Germany for protection, and Germany was eager to comply. As it turns out, the German Kaiser Wilhelm II was looking for an opportunity to prove Germany's role as a world power, and a fight on behalf of Austria-Hungary might be just (46) <u>the opportunity he was looking for</u>. As the alliances lined up, it took only a declaration of war to turn the one event in Sarajevo into a world-changing conflict. Austria-Hungary declared war on Serbia on July 28, 1914. (47) <u>However</u>, Russia announced its support of Serbia. With Russia in the ring, Germany leaped to Austria-Hungary's defense. From there, the dominos began to fall.

France was an ally of Russia. With its proximity to Germany and Austria-Hungary, France declared war on those nations. (48) <u>Germany returned the favor, by invading Belgium</u> in order to reach Paris as quickly as possible. Britain had a longstanding agreement to protect France, as well as Belgium, and thus declared war on Germany. Britain's involvement resulted in the involvement of her far-flung colonies – Canada, South Africa, India, Australia, and New Zealand. Japan had an alliance with Britain and followed by declaring war on Germany. Italy attempted to avoid war for (49) <u>as long as possible, despite alliances with Austria-Hungary and Germany, by pleading a clause</u> in the treaty. According to Italy, this treaty required participation only in the event that her allies were in a defensive position instead of an offensive one. Since both Germany and Austria-Hungary were responsible for the initial declarations, Italy claimed neutrality. (50) <u>This did not last for long, but Italy chose to join the war</u> in May of 1915 by siding with Britain and France instead of her former allies.

38.

    a. June, of 1914
    b. June 1914
    c. June of 1914
    d. June of, 1914

39.

    a. Bosnia Herzegovina in 1909 a move that angered the nearby Kingdom of Serbia
    b. Bosnia Herzegovina in 1909, a move that angered the nearby Kingdom of Serbia
    c. Bosnia Herzegovina in 1909 that angered the nearby Kingdom of Serbia
    d. Bosnia Herzegovina in 1909, since that angered the nearby Kingdom of Serbia

40.

    a. it's
    b. its
    c. its'
    d. its's

62

41.

    a. an isolated, albeit tragic, event in history, ultimately set in motion

    b. an isolated, albeit tragic event in history ultimately set in motion

    c. an isolated, albeit tragic event in history, ultimately set in motion

    d. an isolated, albeit tragic, event in history ultimately set in motion

42.

    a. demanded retribution from Serbia, and even accused the Serbian government

    b. demanded retribution from Serbia and was even accusing the Serbian government

    c. demanded retribution from Serbia, even accused the Serbian government

    d. demanded retribution from Serbia and even accused the Serbian government

43.

    a. if justice were denied

    b. if justice was denied

    c. if justice were being denied

    d. if justice had been denied

44.

    a. empires' war

    b. empires war

    c. empire's war

    d. empire's war's

45.

    a. long time

    b. long-time

    c. long:time

    d. long—time

46.

    a. the opportunity he was looking for

    b. the opportunity that he was looking for

    c. the opportunity for which he was looking

    d. the opportunity he looked for

47.

    a. Surprisingly

    b. In response

    c. With this in mind

    d. Moreover

48.

    a. Germany returned the favor, by invading Belgium

    b. Germany returned the favor invading Belgium

    c. Germany invaded Belgium and returned the favor

    d. Germany returned the favor by invading Belgium

49.

    a. as long as possible, despite alliances with Austria-Hungary and Germany, by pleading a clause
    b. as long as possible despite alliances with Austria-Hungary and Germany, by pleading a clause
    c. as long as possible despite alliances with Austria-Hungary and Germany by pleading a clause
    d. as long as possible, despite alliances with Austria-Hungary and Germany by pleading a clause

50.

    a. This did not last for long, but Italy chose to join the war
    b. This did not last for long, and Italy chose to join the war
    c. This did not last for long, or Italy chose to join the war
    d. This did not last for long, yet Italy chose to join the war

Questions 51-60 pertain to the following excerpt of four paragraphs:

During the 17th century, colonists from Europe arrived in the New World in a variety of circumstances. The cost of crossing the Atlantic (51) <u>was high and many European colonists</u> could not afford it. At the same time, the prospects in the New World were tempting, and colonists sought out alternative options to purchasing a passage on a ship to America. One of these alternatives was that of indentured servitude, which made up nearly (52) <u>80 percent of the European relocation, and ultimately established a strong labor force</u> in the New World.

The indentured servitude began with a signed contract, and the contract laid out the obligations that the servant would have upon arriving in America. The contract generally required a commitment of anywhere from three to seven years from the servant. In exchange, (53) <u>the farmer or shop owner, who hired the indentured servant</u> would provide room and board at no charge. The servant would then serve the required number of years, after which he or she would be free. (54) <u>Without doubt</u>, the indentured servant did not have much of a chance to save up money during the period of servitude, because the servant did not earn money during the time (55) <u>he or she were indentured</u>. Indentured servants did, however, earn valuable information about the farm or business for which they worked, and they could put this information to good use once the period of servitude was over.

One reason the indentured servant was so popular in America was due to the opportunities that were available to those already there. Free farmers and workers had little trouble establishing and working farms or small businesses of (56) <u>there own</u>, so the owners of larger farms and shops struggled to find free workers willing to take the lower wages that were available to them. Farmers and shop owners could purchase slaves, but the cost of slaves could also be high, and the idea of slavery repulsed many. Instead, these (57) <u>farmers and shop owners chose hiring indentured servants</u>.

The indentured servant has often been compared to the slave and the apprentice, but there are some distinct differences. (58) <u>Slaves were owned for life, could only be freed</u> if their owners chose to give them their independence. Apprentices served for a stated period of time, like indentured servants, but they were usually not (59) <u>immigrant's</u> from Europe but rather young people born in the colonies. The apprentice typically came from a poor family that was unable to support the child and chose (60) <u>to apprentice him (and, in some rare cases, her) to a business owner</u> in order to learn the business for a future career.

51.

  a. was high and many European colonists
  b. was high, many European colonists
  c. was high, and many European colonists
  d. was high; and many European colonists

52.

  a. 80 percent of the European relocation, and ultimately established a strong labor force
  b. 80 percent of the European relocation and ultimately established a strong labor force
  c. 80 percent of the European relocation – ultimately established a strong labor force
  d. 80 percent of the European relocation and ultimately establishing a strong labor force

53.

  a. the farmer or shop owner, who hired the indentured servant
  b. the farmer or shop owner; who hired the indentured servant
  c. the farmer or shop owner, that hired the indentured servant
  d. the farmer or shop owner who hired the indentured servant

54.

  a. Without doubt
  b. At the same time
  c. In the same way
  d. Furthermore

55.

  a. he or she were indentured
  b. he or she were being indentured
  c. he or she was indentured
  d. he and she were indentured

56.

  a. there own
  b. they're own
  c. their own
  d. they owned

57.

  a. farmers and shop owners chose hiring indentured servants
  b. farmers and shop owners chose the hiring of indentured servants
  c. farmers and shop owners chose hired indentured servants
  d. farmers and shop owners chose to hire indentured servants

58.

  a. Slaves were owned for life, could only be freed
  b. Slaves were owned for life and could only be freed
  c. Slaves were owned for life, they could only be freed
  d. Slaves were owned for life, and could only be freed

59.

    a. immigrant's
    b. immigrants'
    c. immigrant
    d. immigrants

60.

    a. to apprentice him (and, in some rare cases, her) to a business owner
    b. to apprentice him, and, in some rare cases, her, to a business owner
    c. to apprentice him and, in some rare cases, her, to a business owner
    d. to apprentice him and in some rare cases her to a business owner

Questions 61-70 pertain to the following excerpt of four paragraphs:

In 1559, the English Parliament passed the (61) <u>act of uniformity</u>, setting the religious standards by which all Englishmen and Englishwomen would be judged. Under this act, the Church of England became preeminent, and all citizens were legally required to attend weekly services. What is more, the Act of Uniformity added a fine of 12 pence for any citizen (62) <u>failed to attend a service, Parliament required all Anglican churches</u> to incorporate prayers from the Book of Common Prayer. The reason for such strict obligations was the result of the multiple changes that England had experienced during the reigns of Henry VIII, Edward VI, and Mary I. After (63) <u>Henry's daughter and Edward and Mary's sister Elizabeth I</u> ascended the throne, she attempted create stability with the Act of Uniformity, making a final statement about England's religious choices and requiring all citizens to follow.

While many English citizens sighed with relief at the solidification of (64) <u>religious life in England others objected strongly to the changes</u> that they felt went against their conscience. In particular, members of a group known as Dissenters, or Separatists, began to protest what they viewed as the corruption within the Church of England and the similarity between the Anglican Church and the Roman Catholic Church. At first, they attempted to initiate reform within the church and purge it of what they viewed as (65) <u>'popish'</u> practices. They ultimately failed, and as persecution increased within England they sought opportunities to escape and make a new life for themselves.

At first, the Separatists looked for opportunities within the Netherlands, which offered religious freedom for Protestants during the 16th and 17th centuries. They traveled first to the Dutch cities of (66) <u>Amsterdam, and Leiden</u> in the early 1600s but found that they ultimately struggled to adapt their English ways to a life and a language that was foreign to them in the Netherlands. (67) <u>On the other hand</u>, many of the Separatists worried about the influences that Dutch society would have on their children. Life among the Dutch had fewer moral restrictions than the (68) <u>Separatists were comfortable accepting, and they began looking for another opportunity</u> to escape the restrictions of English religious life while still being able to live as Englishmen and Englishwomen.

The opportunity presented itself in the form of the New World settlement in Virginia. England already had a growing settlement at Jamestown, and the Separatists looked to establish a settlement of their own (69) <u>near this – but not too near this</u>, of course, to avoid too much infiltration of the crown's religious and political system. In 1620, the group that became known as the Pilgrims set sail for the New World in the *Mayflower* and headed for America. A storm altered the direction of the ship, and the Pilgrims ultimately landed north of their intended destination. They ended up on Cape Cod in (70) <u>modern day Massachusetts</u> and there established what would be known as Plymouth Colony.

61.

    a. act of uniformity
    b. Act of uniformity
    c. Act of Uniformity
    d. act of Uniformity

62.

    a. failed to attend a service, Parliament required all Anglican churches
    b. failed to attend a service, and Parliament required all Anglican churches
    c. failed to attend a service; Parliament required all Anglican churches
    d. failed to attend a service, but Parliament required all Anglican churches

63.

    a. Henry's daughter and Edward and Mary's sister Elizabeth I
    b. Henry's daughter, and Edward and Mary's sister Elizabeth I
    c. Henry's daughter [and Edward and Mary's sister] Elizabeth I
    d. Henry's daughter (and Edward and Mary's sister) Elizabeth I

64.

    a. religious life in England others objected strongly to the changes
    b. religious life in England – others objected strongly to the changes
    c. religious life in England, others objected strongly to the changes
    d. religious life in England; others objected strongly to the changes

65.

    a. 'popish'
    b. "popish"
    c. " 'popish' "
    d. – popish –

66.

    a. Amsterdam, and Leiden
    b. Amsterdam, Leiden
    c. Amsterdam-Leiden
    d. Amsterdam and Leiden

67.

    a. On the other hand
    b. At the same time
    c. Additionally
    d. Consequently

68.

   a. Separatists were comfortable accepting, and they began looking for another opportunity
   b. Separatists were comfortable accepting and they began looking for another opportunity
   c. Separatists were comfortable accepting: they began looking for another opportunity
   d. Separatists were comfortable accepting, they began looking for another opportunity

69.

   a. near this – but not too near this
   b. near this, but not too near this
   c. near this but not too near this
   d. near this; but not too near this

70.

   a. modern day Massachusetts
   b. modern day-Massachusetts
   c. modern-day-Massachusetts
   d. modern-day Massachusetts

Written Essay

You will have 30 minutes to write an essay on an assigned topic. Sample topics are provided below. Choose one.

As you create your essay, you should present and support your point of view. Your writing will be evaluated on the quality of the writing and not on your opinion. A good essay will have an organized structure, clear thesis, and logical supporting details. Ensure that you are presenting your topic in a way that appeals to your target audience. Use clear and appropriate word choice throughout. Ensure that grammar, punctuation, and spelling are correct. Your response can be of any length.

1. The federal government has long struggled with the issue of income tax. Many people feel that government programs require the collection of an income tax, and that it makes sense to collect more tax money from the wealthier members of society. Other people declare that is unfair to penalize individuals for being successful, and suggest that the same amount of income tax be applied to all citizens. These people further suggest that overtaxing the wealthiest members of society actually has a deleterious effect on the economy for everyone, because it discourages investment and the creation of new jobs.

2. A state government has decided that rather than maintain tollbooths and employees to generate funds for road improvement, it would be more efficient to simply increase the state income tax. Proponents of this plan declare that even those individuals who do not drive on the toll road are the recipients of goods transported there. They also suggest that money can be saved by reducing the number of state employees and maintenance on aging toll offices.

Answer Key and Explanations

Job Knowledge

1. D: Anthropology is the study of human social relationships and the analysis of cultural characteristics. Economists study how societies use resources and distribute goods. Political science is the study of government and political institutions. Psychologists focus on mental functions and human behavior.

2. C: Exploration between the 15th and 17th centuries resulted in contact between European cultures and many previously unknown or little-known cultures. Navigation techniques improved, food and other goods were imported, and the New World began to be settled. Rather than declining in influence, England became a more prominent imperial power during this era.

3. B: Although both Israel and Saudi Arabia border on the Gulf of Aqaba, Jordan stands between Israel and its giant neighbor to the southeast.

4. B: Three times the size of the continental United States, Africa contains a surprisingly small percentage of the world population. The continent is divided roughly in half by the equator. The rain forest makes up about 15 percent of central Africa.

5. C: Johnson exerted his presidential power to advance the Great Society agenda and to enact major civil rights legislation. He also conducted a war in Vietnam without Congressional declaration. Jefferson, Hoover, and Bush were all outspoken advocates of limiting the role of government, including the executive branch.

6. C: Physical geography focuses on processes and patterns in the natural environment. What people eat in any given geographic region is largely dependent on such environmental factors as climate and the availability of arable land. Religion, family, and language may all be affected by geographical factors, but they are not as immediately affected as dietary preferences.

7. D: Lying between the Tigris and Euphrates rivers, the Mesopotamian region gave rise to many prominent cultures. Today, the land belongs mainly to Iraq while extending to parts of northeastern Syria, southeastern Turkey, and southwestern Iran.

8. B: The North American Free Trade Agreement was established in 1994 by the United States, Canada, and Mexico in an effort to minimize trade barriers among the continent's three nations.

9. B: A strict constructionist, Jefferson argued that that the Constitution did not make any provision for the creation of a federal bank. Jefferson was a leader of the Democratic-Republicans who opposed the establishment of a powerful central government. He believed that the Bank would give an unfair advantage to the more industrial northern states.

10. B: Lower interest rates allow banks to lend out more money, which serves to stimulate consumer spending. Increased spending tends to raise, not lower, prices. The Federal Reserve Board is not actively involved in international trade. The fear of inflation usually leads to a raise in interest rates.

11. A: In 1985, Mikhail Gorbachev's programs of "glasnost," or openness, and "perestroika," or economic restructuring, led to an increase in free speech and free enterprise throughout the Soviet Union. By 1991, these reforms had led to the collapse of Communist power in Russia and the

70

dissolution of the Soviet Union. Russia and the other newly independent states that comprised the former Soviet Union suffered great economic hardship following the breakup. With the collapse of the Soviet Union as a world power, the Cold War that began after World War II came to an end. The bloody conflict in Bosnia (1992-1995) was caused in part by the weakening of Communist control in Yugoslavia at the end of the Cold War.

12. D: In the Dred Scott decision of 1857, the Court ruled that no slave or descendent of slaves could ever be a United States citizen. It also declared the Missouri Compromise of 1820 to be unconstitutional, clearing the way for the expansion of slavery in new American territories. This ruling pleased Southerners and outraged the North further dividing the nation and setting the stage for war.

13. A: Maine was the northern part of the Massachusetts Bay colony and subsequently part of the Commonwealth of Massachusetts. It became a state in 1820 as a result of the Missouri Compromise.

14. D: In his extremely influential pamphlet *Common Sense*, Paine argued persuasively against all forms of monarchy and aristocracy. He advocated the formation of a republic that derives its power exclusively from the governed. While the European writers also advocated government that derives its authority from the people, none went as far as Paine in proposing the total abolition of the traditional noble classes.

15. D: Without the power of taxation, the new federal government had to rely on the states to provide the money needed to wage war against England and to pay the huge national debt accrued during the Revolution. The power to raise revenues through taxation was an essential feature of the subsequent Constitution.

16. A: Article II of the Constitution gives the House of Representatives the sole power of impeachment and the Senate the sole power to convict. The Chief Justice of the United States is empowered to preside over the Senate trial of a President.

17. B: Marx's focus in *The Communist Manifesto* (1848) and *Das Kapital* (1867) was on the inevitable conflict between the working class and the capitalists who own the means of production. He identified these two opposing forces as the proletariat and the bourgeoisie.

18. A: Checks and balances prevent any branch of the government from running roughshod over the other two. Separation of powers refers to the distribution of specific powers among the three branches of government. Judicial review is the power of the courts to overturn legislative or executive acts that are deemed unconstitutional. Advice and consent is the power to advise the President, ratify treaties, and confirm nominations, which is granted to the Senate in Article II of the Constitution.

19. D: The process of overriding a Presidential veto is described in Article I, Section 7, of the Constitution. A veto can only be overridden by a two-thirds vote in both houses of Congress.

20. D: Madison proposed nineteen amendments to the first Congress in 1789 twelve of which were sent to the states and ten officially ratified in 1791. Neither Adams nor Jefferson was present at the Constitutional Convention.

21. B: Shared, or concurrent, powers are those powers held by both the states and the federal government. While the Constitution specifically grants Congress the exclusive power to coin money, it does not specifically forbid the states from building roads, collecting taxes, and establishing courts.

22. D: While all social science is concerned to some extent with how societies make use of whatever resources are available to them, the production and distribution of goods is of primary concern to the economist.

23. D: According to the Tenth Amendment to the Constitution: "The powers not delegated to the United States by the Constitution, nor prohibited by it to the States, are reserved to the States respectively, or to the people." As the regulation of education and marriage are neither delegated to the federal government nor prohibited to the states, they are powers reserved for the states.

24. B: Article I of the Constitution mandates the taking of a census every ten years. The purpose was to be sure that each state was proportionately represented in Congress according to its population as specified in the Constitution. Census data is also used to allocate federal funding for various programs and for shaping economic policies. Individual data collected by the U.S. Bureau of the Census is kept confidential for seventy-two years and does not affect income tax rates. Every state has two seats in the Senate regardless of population.

25. A: The First Amendment addresses freedom of speech, assembly, religion and the freedom of the press. A speedy trial is covered in the Sixth Amendment, cruel and unusual punishment in the Eighth Amendment, and search and seizure in the Fourth Amendment.

26. C: The FDIC and the SEC were both New Deal agencies created by the FDR administration in response to the stock market crash and bank failures of the Great Depression era. Both agencies still play an important role in maintaining public confidence in the nation's fundamental economic institutions.

27. C: Mexico is the second largest producer of oil in the Western Hemisphere while Venezuela has the largest oil reserves in South America. Bolivia, Guatemala, and Uruguay are not petroleum-producing nations.

28. B: Shared, or concurrent, powers are those powers held by both the states and the federal government. These include taxation, borrowing money, establishing courts, and making and enforcing laws. Implied powers are those assumed by the federal government based on the "elastic clause" in Article I of the Constitution. Expressed, or enumerated, powers are those specifically granted to the federal government in Article I, Section 8 of the Constitution—e.g., the right to coin money, declare war, and regulate interstate and foreign commerce. Reserved powers are reserved exclusively to the states.

29. D: A contingency approach is built around the idea that the context in which an organization operates affects the effectiveness of the organization's form. The four contingencies that research shows affect organizational structure are size, strategy, technology, and environment.

30. B: The Equal Pay Act of 1963 sought to eliminate wage disparities based on gender and guarantees equal pay for men and women doing equal work.

31. B: Legitimate power comes from the belief of employees that their supervisors have the right to ask things of them. Coercive power comes from the threat of negative consequences. Expert power comes from the expertise, or richer knowledge and information, that a leader possesses. Referent power comes from the desire of an employee to be like his/her supervisor.

32. D: Managers average about 20% of their time dealing with conflict.

33. D: All of the answer options can give rise to conflict. Lack of clear definition of roles can create confusion and conflicting expectations; inadequate resources and different goals can create conflict over resources or over focus of effort; and the need to rely on others to complete tasks can create conflict over timing or quality of work.

34. C: The term *richness* describes the quantity and quality of information a medium can convey. The richest medium is face-to-face. In addition to the actual words spoken, face-to-face communication gives the communication receiver information in the form of non-verbal language and vocal inflection.

35. D: *Vertical communication* refers to information sharing between staff in the same unit. *Horizontal communication* refers to information sharing between staff at the same level. *Diagonal communication* refers to the sharing of information between people in a company who are neither in the same unit nor at the same level.

36. D: Group decision-making offers advantages and disadvantages. One of the disadvantages of this decision-making style is the fact that individuals in groups bring with them their own independent thoughts, opinions, and information. Although this is an advantage for the group in terms of having a larger pool of information resources, it also creates additional work and time pressure from having a greater amount of information to consider.

37. A: *Human capital* refers to the stock of knowledge, skills, and abilities held by a company's workforce and enabling them to perform labor to produce economic value.

38. A: Negligent hiring suits result from the application of the theory of negligence to the employment context. Essentially, an employer can be liable for injuries caused to their employees by other employees if the injury resulted from being unfit for the job by someone whose unfitness the employer knew or should have known of.

39. D: In total, the man is buying 5 steak dinners (one for himself and 4 for his friends). To find the total amount he will have to spend, multiply the cost of one dinner ($15.99) by the number of dinners purchased (5): $15.99 * 5 = $79.95

40. D: First, calculate the amount of interest that will be earned on the first account: $329 * 0.04 = $13.16

Then, add this amount to the amount that was already in the account:

$13.16 + $329 = $342.16

Next, calculate the amount of interest that will be earned on the second account:

$921 * 0.07 = $64.47

Then, add this amount to the amount that was already in the account:

$64.47 + $921 = $985.47

Finally, add the two totals together: $342.16 + $985.47 = $1327.63

41. A: First, figure out how many bags of potatoes would be sold if six bags of onions were sold. The ratio of onions sold to potatoes sold is 6: 1. So, if he sells 12 bags of onions, we must divide this number by six to get the number of bags of potatoes sold: 12 / 6 = 2

Then, use this number to figure out how many bags of carrots he would sell:

The problem tells us that he sells two bags of potatoes for each bag of carrots. Therefore, he would sell 1 bag of carrots if he sold 12 bags of onions.

42. C: First, calculate how much he had at the end of the first week: $150 – $45 = $105

Since he tripled his money, it is then necessary to multiply this value by 3:

$105 * 3 = $315

43. B: To figure out how much the woman pays in income tax each year, calculate 36% of $65,000: $65,000 * 0.36 = $23,400

44. D: First, calculate how many girls there will be after 10 more join the class: 13 + 10 = 23

Then, express the number of girls compared to boys as a ratio: 23 : 15.

45. D: To calculate the man's total weekly salary, find the total amount he earns at his three jobs: $500 + $65 + $175 = $740

46. D: In Charles Darwin's theory of evolution, natural selection is the mechanism by which species evolve. Darwin posited that there is a variation of characteristics in individual organisms within a species. Some characteristics better equip individual organisms to survive and reproduce. When these organisms reproduce, their offspring are likely to inherit those advantageous characteristics. Over time, the species itself may evolve based on the widespread inheritance of such characteristics with survival value. Therefore, natural selection is concerned with the evolution of species as a whole, rather than adaptation of individual organisms. This eliminates choice B. While environmental pressures can play a role in natural selection, natural selection does not describe the diversity of such pressures. This eliminates choice A. Answer C can be rejected because Darwin did not believe characteristics acquired during an organism's lifetime were inherited.

47. A: Russian's involvement in World War I brought social tension in Russia to a head. Contributing factors included military defeats and civilian suffering. Prior to Russia entering the war, Russian factory workers could legally strike, but during the war, it was illegal for them to act collectively. This eliminates answer C. Protests continued during World War I, and the Russian government was overthrown in 1917. This eliminates answer D. Answer B can be rejected because World War I did not go well for the Russian Army; Nicholas III, therefore, had no successes upon which to capitalize.

48. D: As a result of the Spanish-American War, the United States became a more powerful nation. At the war's end, Spain ceded Guam and Puerto Rico to the United States, and the United States purchased the Philippines for $20 million. Answer A can be rejected because, though the United States Navy represented itself very well throughout the war, the United States Army was plagued by inefficiency. Answer B can be rejected because Spain was the first nation in the conflict to issue a formal declaration of war. This is true in spite of the fact that Spain's declaration of war came in part as a response to American actions. Answer C can be rejected because the sinking of the Maine did not cast doubts on the U.S. Navy. Rather, the U.S. Navy defeated Spanish ships rather handily.

49. A: In exchange for the removal of Soviet Cuban missile launching sites, which were under construction at the time of the crisis, President Khrushchev sought a pledge from the United States that the United States would not invade Cuba. Khrushchev also demanded that the United States close its missile launching sites located in Turkey, not on an island off the Soviet coast. This eliminates option B. The Soviet Union did not demand either an apology from the United States as a condition for the removal of the launching sites, or negotiations regarding the production of nuclear weapons. This eliminates options C and D.

50. B: After World War I, the United States passed the Immigration Act of 1924, which regulated the number of immigrants in part according to their national origin. The United States sought to avoid the problems of Europe and other nations by limiting the number of foreigners who entered the United States. Option A can be rejected because quite soon after World War I, both inflation and unemployment were significant problems in the United States. Option C can be rejected because in the years immediately following World War I, the United States did not built its navy even to the extent allowed by treaty. Finally, option D can be rejected because after World War I, the United States made arrangements for the U.S. to have access to oil in Colombia and in Middle Eastern countries.

51. C: The 1944 G.I. Bill offered several significant benefits for U.S. U.S. veterans. These included economic assistance for veterans to attend college, mortgage subsidies, and unemployment benefits. Over a million veterans took advantage of the opportunity to attend college, and many homes were built with support provided by the G.I. Bill. This increase in home ownership and the availability of higher education contributed to the creation of a new middle class. The Bill did not offer veterans specific incentives for staying in the military after World War II; this eliminates option A. It did not offer free housing for veterans; this eliminates option B. Finally the Bill did not privilege veterans in the work force; this eliminates option D.

52. D: The Ka'ba is an ancient structure Muslims consider holy; it was purportedly built by Abraham. The Ka'ba's location in Mecca is the central reason for Mecca's importance to Muslims. Although Muhammad was born in Mecca, that fact is not the primary reason for Mecca's importance in Islam; the location of the Ka'ba is more important. This eliminates option A. Option C can be rejected because Muhammad fled from Mecca to Medina in 622 A.D., not the other way around. Option B can be rejected because Muslims believe the Second Coming will occur in Damascus, not Mecca.

53. B: According to Buddhism, life is full of suffering. However, by following the Noble Eightfold Path, the path of moral living, it is possible to end suffering. Samsara, the cycle of birth, death, and rebirth, is an important concept in Buddhism, but it is not the Noble Eightfold Path; therefore option A can be rejected. Regarding option C, there are Precepts in Buddhism that offer a guide to Buddhist ethical behavior; these are related to the Noble Eightfold Path, but they are not the same; this eliminates option C. Finally, while self is an illusion according to Buddhist doctrine, this view is not the substance of the Noble Eightfold Path. This eliminates option D.

54. A: In a departure from classical painting, Cubists painted their subjects as though from multiple perspectives rather than from a single perspective, as though to reflect the increasingly complex world of the 20th century. This approach to painting included paintings of the human body; the paintings therefore sometimes seemed to distort the human body rather than elevate it or regard it as sacrosanct. This eliminates option B. Cubism favored rationality over emotion in that it involved breaking up subjects along geometric planes; this eliminates option C. Finally, option D can be rejected because Cubist paintings often utilized tame, mild colors, rather than bright, vivid ones.

55. A: World population growth has significantly affected global deforestation, as forests have been cleared for agricultural use, livestock, and timber harvesting. World population growth has not lead to increased biodiversity. Global biodiversity has actually shrunk in response to humanity's exponential population growth; this eliminates option B. Similarly, ocean dead zones – regions featuring low concentrations of oxygen – have grown in the last decades rather than shrunk; this eliminates option C. Finally, although there have been mass extinction events throughout earth history (such as those involving dinosaurs), they are not linked to world population growth; this eliminates option D.

56. D: Under the War Powers Act of 1973, the President can send combat troops to battle (or to an area where hostilities are imminent) for only 60 days, with the possibility of extending this period of time to 90 days. In order to keep deployed troops in place (or to send additional troops) after this period of time has elapsed, the President must seek Congressional approval, either in the form of a mandate or in the form of a declaration of war. Option A can be eliminated because Congress was responsible for approving war-related funding prior to the War Powers Act, which did not affect this responsibility. Neither option B nor option C accurately describes the importance of the War Powers Act.

57. C: A federalist system of government is a government under which power is shared by a central authority and sub-components of the federation. In the United States in particular, power is shared by the federal government and the individual states. Option A, that the legislative branch consists of two representative bodies (the House of Representatives and the Senate) is true, of course, but does not describe a uniquely federalist structure. Rather, it describes the concept of bicameralism. Option A may thus be eliminated. Option B, likewise, describes different types of democracy but not federalism. B can thus be eliminated. Regarding option D, this statement is also true (the U.S. Constitution shapes national legislation) but it is not a descriptive statement of the federalist system because the statement makes no mention that power is shared by the states.

58. C: The main subject matter of civic responsibility is a person's responsibilities as a citizen. By contrast, the main subject matter of personal responsibility is one's responsibilities as a person. For example, keeping a promise to a friend is often a matter of personal responsibility because such a duty arises from the friendship. Serving on a jury when called to do so is an example of civic responsibility because such a duty arises from the person's citizenship. None of the other options given accurately describe the main subject matter of civic responsibility. For example, while a journalist might see accurate reporting of government actions as his or her civic responsibility, such reporting is not the main subject matter of civic responsibility, and is also a responsibility that arises from that journalist's employment. Similar reasoning applies to a person's responsibilities as a government worker. This eliminates options A and D. Civic responsibility does not primarily concern inter-government relations; this eliminates option B.

59. B: The Electoral College officially elects the President and the Vice President. The number of electors, or Electoral College members, allotted to a state is equal to that state's total number of U.S. Senators and U.S. Representatives. A state with two U.S. Senators and one U.S. Representative, for example, would have three electors in the Electoral College. Because every state has two U.S. Senators and at least one U.S. Representative, every state has at least 3 electors in the Electoral College. Option B is the only option that correctly describes how a state's number of Electoral College voters is determined; neither the number of counties in a state, nor the number of State Secretaries is relevant to this number.

60. D: In a parliamentary form of government, the executive branch is essentially a committee of the legislative branch. This is the only answer that correctly describes the relation between the executive branch and another branch of the government. The executive branch is neither a committee of the judicial branch, nor is it appointed by the judicial branch; this eliminates options B and C. The executive branch does not appoint members of the legislative branch; this eliminates option A. In the parliamentary government in Great Britain, for example, the legislature elects the Prime Minister, and the members of the Prime Minister's Cabinet are also selected from members of the legislative branch (either the House of Commons or the House of Lords).

English Expression

1. A: The phrase is correct with the hyphen. The hyphen connects the two words, uniting them into a single adjective that modifies "sermon." The expression is incorrect (as well as misspelled) with the words joined together. The slash is also incorrect, because there is no either-or option with "now" and "famous." (That is to say, the sentence does not read the same way without with either "now" or "famous.")

2. C: The double quotation marks correctly identify "Sinners in the Hands of an Angry God" as the formal title of a sermon. The single quotation marks are only correct in standard American usage for a quote within a quote. The comma makes little sense in the title, and there is nothing about the context of the sentence that would suggest the need for a comma after the word "Sinners."

3. B: The commas around the expression offer a slight pause in the reading of the sentence without breaking the overall flow of the sentence. The lack of commas and the comma only after "Edwards" make the sentence read awkwardly. The commas around "and thus Calvinists" is not necessarily incorrect, but these commas alone are not enough, since the expression starting with "arguing from" is the larger phrase that needs a pause.

4. A: The sentence reads comfortably without punctuation, so it is not necessary to place any punctuation before the word "who." The comma creates a pause where no pause is needed, and the colon and semicolon create fragments.

5. B: The apostrophe before the letter "s" indicates singular possession, which is indicated by the context of the sentence. The lack of the apostrophe and the apostrophes located elsewhere are incorrect and not appropriate to the context of the sentence.

6. C: The word "effects" is the correct usage in this context. The noun usage of "affects" is not correct in this case, and both "affecting" and "effecting" make little sense in the sentence.

7. C: No comma is necessary, because the conjunction "and" joins two verbs instead of two independent clauses. The comma does not make the sentence incorrect, but it is also unnecessary and does little to improve the flow of thought within the sentence. The lack of the conjunction makes the sentence read more awkwardly, and the semicolon creates a fragment.

8. B: The parentheses indicate a side thought that is relevant to the sentence but does not belong within the natural flow of thought. The lack of parentheses breaks up the flow of thought awkwardly. The brackets indicate an authorial comment that does not fit the context of the sentence. The exclamation point also makes little sense in the context of the sentence.

9. D: The comma creates the necessary pause without breaking up the flow of the sentence. The semicolon and the period create fragments, while the dash is not appropriate since the material that follows has little dramatic impact on the sentence.

10. C: The commas are accurate and set off the transitional expression effectively. The single comma creates awkwardness rather than clarity. The colon makes no sense and creates an uncomfortable flow of thought within the sentence.

11. C: No comma is necessary before the conjunction, because it joins two items in a series instead of two independent clauses. The conjunction "but" makes little sense in the context of the sentence, and the comma alone creates an awkward reading of the sentence.

12. B: No punctuation is necessary between the words "single" and "sense," because "single" is an adjective modifying "sense."

13. D: The comma before "as well" is correct, because it indicates the start of a dependent clause and offers a slight pause in the sentence. The colon and the semicolon create fragments, and the lack of a comma makes the ideas run into each other uncomfortably.

14. A: The sentence is correct with the parentheses, because the parentheses offer information that is useful but that needs to be set off for the reader. The comma would only be correct if there was a conjunction such as "or" to indicate another or clarifying version of the expression. The brackets are not correct in this context and should only be included with an authorial side note, and the dashes, while not technically incorrect, are not justified in the context of the sentence.

15. D: No comma is necessary before "as well," because the flow of the sentence does not call for a pause here. The semicolon and the period create fragments.

16. A: Again, the sentence is correct as it is. The comma is correctly placed before the coordinating conjunction "but." A comma is necessary before a coordinating conjunction, so the lack of the comma reflects incorrect punctuation usage. The semicolon and the period, while not inaccurate, are not necessary since the sentence already has a coordinating conjunction.

17. C: Correct usage places the period within the quotation marks. (Periods and commas always belong within quotation marks.) The exclamation point is not required in the context of the sentence, and the single quotation marks are incorrect for standard quotations.

18. B: The parentheses offer a clarification and are appropriate in this usage. The colon and the semicolon create fragments, and the lack of any punctuation makes the ideas run into each other awkwardly.

19. B: This is another use of the comma before the coordinating conjunction, so answer choice B is correct. The comma always belongs before the coordinating conjunction instead of after it, so answer choice C is incorrect. The period without the coordinating conjunction is not necessarily incorrect, but the sentence reads more comfortably with the addition of "so" (to create a cause-and-effect relationship). The comma alone is a comma splice and creates a run-on sentence.

20. D: Answer choice D accurately sets off the expression "also known as the Mormon Church" with commas. Commas are needed on both sides of the expression, so a single comma on either side is incorrect, and the lack of commas creates an awkward flow of thought in the sentence.

21. C: The comma signals the start of a dependent clause that starts with "which." The colon and the semicolon create fragments, and the comma after "which" is not necessary (particularly since there is no comma after "to this day" to set off that expression).

22. B: The comma sets off the dependent clause that begins with "where." The period creates a fragment. The dash, which should indicate a somewhat dramatic statement, has no clear place in the context of the sentence. The removal of "where" and the substitution of "and" does nothing to improve the flow of thought and is thus unnecessary.

23. D: Since the names of the other movements are capitalized (Abolition and Prohibition), capitalizing Women's Suffrage is appropriate in this context. The capitalization of either word, but not both, makes little sense in the context of capitalizing the name of a movement.

24. D: Since the previous expression, starting with "hence," is placed in parentheses, the statement starting with "explaining" should also be in parentheses. Any other use of punctuation to offset this expression conflicts with the parallelism of the sentence and is incorrect.

25. A: The sentence is correct as it is punctuated. A comma belongs after an introductory phrase, so answer choice A is accurate. The opening phrase requires a slight pause after it, so the lack of the comma is incorrect, and the semicolon and the period create fragments.

26. D: The comma creates a slight pause before the word "with," allowing for a smoother flow of thought within the sentence. The semicolon and the period create fragments, and the dash is unnecessary in the context of the sentence.

27. B: No apostrophe is necessary, because the word "colonists" is plural instead of possessive. All uses of the apostrophe are incorrect and create confusion in the sentence.

28. A: A comma belongs before the word "because" when it functions as a coordinating conjunction. The lack of the comma makes the ideas run together awkwardly, and the comma after the word "because" is unnecessary without the clear need for a pause in the sentence. The period creates a fragment.

29. C: The best opening expression is "In other words," because the author is explaining or clarifying the information that was in the previous sentence. "On the other hand" creates a contrast that does not exist in the context of the sentence. "For example" makes little sense, because the author is restating instead of providing a specific example. "Additionally" is inappropriate, because the author is clarifying previously stated information instead of adding new information.

30. B: The colon is correct, because the author is expanding on or defining the information that came before. The author notes that there was a frustrating issue developing, and this issue was the lack of colonial representation in Parliament. The period is not necessarily incorrect, but it creates too much of a break between the two ideas and is thus not as effective as the colon. The comma alone is a comma splice and creates a run-on sentence, and the comma with the coordinating conjunction joins the sentences awkwardly

31. C: The comma with the coordinating conjunction "so" offers the necessary cause-and-effect relationship between the two independent clauses. The lack of punctuation and the comma alone (comma splice) create fragments, and the use of the conjunction "but" is unnecessary without a clear sense of contrast in the sentence.

32. C: Answer choice C adjusts the word order to remove the passive tense, which is always to be avoided when possible. The colon creates a fragment and therefore cannot be correct.

33. C: No punctuation is necessary within this expression, because the conjunction "not only...but also" joins two items in a series instead of two independent clauses. Additionally, the most effective reading of the sentence is "...not only colonists but also the merchants..." The other answer choices add punctuation where it is not necessary or create an awkward reading of the sentence.

34. B: The commas on both sides of the expression set it off just slightly and are correct. The single comma on either side creates an awkward pause before or after the expression (but not before *and* after it, which is acceptable). The dashes do not fit the context of the sentence and are incorrect.

35. D: The conjunction in this case joins two items in a series, so no punctuation is necessary. The use of "or" is simply confusing, given that the author makes it clear the objections came from *both* colonists and British merchants.

36. A: No capitalization or punctuation is necessary here. The phrase "colonial representation" is composed of an adjective and a noun, both of them common instead of proper, so capitalization and/or punctuation is not called for in the context of the sentence.

37. B: The comma indicates a coordinating conjunction that joins two independent clauses, so it is correct. The lack of the comma fails to signal the coordinating conjunction (and thus the start of the new clause). The comma alone splices the two sentences together incorrectly, and the period, while not necessarily inaccurate, is also not necessary.

38. C: The correct usage is "June of 1914," with no punctuation. To use the month and year without the preposition "of," a comma is necessary (i.e., "June, 1914").

39. B: The comma provides a brief pause before the phrase "a move," to improve the flow of thought and avoiding the ideas running into each other awkwardly. The use of "at" instead of "a move" does little to improve the meaning of the sentence, and the use of "since" creates confusion in the context of the sentence. (There is no indication that Austria-Hungary annexed Bosnia Herzegovina in order to anger the Kingdom of Serbia.)

40. B: The word "its," with no punctuation, is the correct usage of the possessive pronoun. The word "it's" is the contraction for "it is," while the apostrophes in "its'" and "it's'" are never correct.

41. D: Answer choice D offers the best punctuation of the sentence, setting off "albeit tragic" with commas but not using any further commas to create pauses in the sentence. The comma after "history" makes little sense in the sentence, and the comma before "albeit tragic" but not after it fail to set off the phrase effectively.

42. D: No punctuation is necessary here, because the conjunction "and" joins two verbs instead of two independent clauses. The shift in the verb, from "accused" to "was even accusing" breaks the parallelism of the sentence, and the lack of the conjunction creates an awkward reading in the sentence.

43. A: Answer choice A is correct, because it uses the subjunctive tense to indicate an event that (within the context of the description in the sentence) has not yet occurred – that is, justice potentially being denied. All other verb usages are incorrect, because they do not fit the context of the sentence.

44. C: The use of "empire" is singular in this case, referring to the Austro-Hungarian Empire. The apostrophe at the end of the word "empires" creates a possessive of a plural word, and that is not called for in the context of the sentence. The lack of the apostrophe cannot be correct, because the word is clearly possessive. The possessive use of "war's" is also incorrect, because the sentence indicates that the word should be plural instead of possessive.

45. B: The hyphen is correct to indicate that the combination of the two words represents a single adjective that modifies the noun "ally." The lack of the hyphen fails to join the words as they should be joined. The colon has no place joining words, and the dash is not correct in this usage, as it also cannot be used to join two words.

46. C: Answer choice C reflects a grammar rule that is not applied too often but it still correct: sentences should not end with prepositions when the preposition can be avoided. Answer choice C avoids placing the preposition at the end without creating any awkwardness. The addition of "that" does nothing to remove the preposition from the end of the sentence, and the switch from "he was looking" to "he looked" makes no difference with the preposition at the end.

47. B: The phrase "In response" is the most effective transitional expression, because it links Germany's declaration of war to Russia's declaration of war. The word "Surprisingly" makes little sense, given the fact that the author previously noted Serbia's connection to Russia. The phrase "With this in mind" does nothing to improve the flow of thought, and "Moreover" makes little sense in the context of the sentence.

48. D: No punctuation is necessary before the word "by" since the expression "by invading Belgium" is a phrase instead of the start of a dependent clause. The removal of "by" creates confusion in the sentence, and the rewording to "Germany invaded Belgium and returned the favor" alters the obvious flow of thought within the sentence.

49. A: The commas set off the phrase "despite alliances with Austria-Hungary and Germany" with slight pauses and thus makes the sentence easier for the reader to follow. The lack of commas or the single commas on either side do nothing to ease the flow of thought and ultimately create confusion.

50. B: The conjunction "and" offers the best way to join the two independent clauses. The conjunctions "but," "or," and "yet" only create confusion within the sentence by failing to clearly establish the relationship between the two clauses.

51. C: The comma is correct before the coordinating conjunction to indicate that the conjunction joins two independent clauses (and thus two sentences). The comma without the coordinating conjunction creates an awkward flow of thought. The semicolon is not necessary with the coordinating conjunction.

52. B: No punctuation is necessary within the sentence, because the conjunction joins two verbs within a single independent clause instead of two independent clauses. The dash is unnecessary in the context of the sentence, and the use of "ultimately establishing" with the conjunction "and" makes little sense in the context of the sentence.

53. D: No punctuation is necessary before the word "who" to signal the dependent clause in this case. The semicolon creates a fragment, and the use of "that" instead of "who" is unnecessary and does nothing to improve the flow of thought within the sentence.

54. B: The phrase "At the same time" is the best opening expression to transition from one sentence to the next, because it indicates a sense of contrast between the ideas. The use of "Without doubt" creates a contextual indication that is not present in the sentences. "In the same way" is akin to "Additionally" and does not belong in the sentence. Similarly, the word "Furthermore" indicates addition and makes no sense in the context of the two sentences.

55. C: The use of "or" indicates that a singular verb is necessary, so "was" is correct to join "his or her." All other uses (with "and") are grammatically incorrect.

81

56. C: The word "their" is a possessive pronoun and is therefore correct in the context of the sentence. The word "there" indicates direction, and the contraction "they're" indicates "they are." The use of "they owned" makes no sense in the context of the sentence.

57. D: The use of the infinitive "to hire" is the best usage in the context of the sentence. The use of "hiring" and "the hiring of" create an awkward flow of thought. The word "hired" makes little sense in the sentence.

58. B: Similar to question 52, no punctuation is necessary because the conjunction joins two verbs within the single independent clause. The comma without the conjunction reduces the effectiveness of the flow of thought. The comma with the word "they" creates a comma splice and therefore a run-on sentence.

59. D: No punctuation in the word "immigrants" indicates correctly that the word is plural instead of possessive. All uses of the apostrophe are inaccurate, and the use of "immigrant" (singular) does not fit the context of the sentence.

60. A: The sentence is correct with the parentheses and with the commas that are within the parentheses. The parentheses set off an authorial comment that is essential but does not necessarily function as the primary material of the sentence. The commas within the parenthetical reference offset the nonessential expression "in some cases." The use of commas alone is not entirely incorrect but creates an awkward amount of commas that can ultimately confuse the readers instead of assisting them. The comma after "her" does not work, because it is the end of an entire expression that needs some punctuation to offset it. The lack of any commas makes it difficult for the reader to appreciate the flow of thought as effectively as possible.

61. C: Because this is the official name of a law, it should be capitalized: Act of Uniformity. The preposition "of" does not need to be capitalized, because it is less than three letters in length. (Longer prepositions – such as "among" may be capitalized in formal names.) All other forms of the name are incorrect without the full capitalization.

62. B: The comma is necessary before the coordinating conjunction, because it signals the start of a new independent clause. The comma without the conjunction is a comma splice and therefore creates a run-on sentence. The semicolon is not grammatically incorrect, but it contributes nothing to the sentence and actually makes the flow of thought more awkward instead of improving it. The conjunction "but" creates a contrast within the sentence and does not fit the context of the sentence.

63. D: The parentheses are effective in the sentence, because they accurately include the information about Elizabeth I's relationship to Edward and Mary without creating too much information within the primary part of the sentence. The comma before "and" creates awkwardness within the sentence by not offsetting both sides of the phrase. The context of the sentence does not call for brackets, because there is nothing about the information to suggest that this is an authorial side instead of a valuable piece of information for the sentence.

64. C: The comma after "England" indicates the end of an introductory clause for the sentence and creates a useful pause for the reader. The lack of the comma makes the ideas run into each other awkwardly. The dash is unnecessary, because the context calls for a basic pause instead of a dramatic break in the sentence. The semicolon creates a fragment.

65. B: The double quotation marks are correct to indicate a statement within quotes – that is, a statement that suggests the comment or opinion from a source (in this case, the way the Separatists viewed the practices of the Anglican Church). The singular quotes and the single quotes within the double quotation marks are incorrect in this usage that requires standard double quotes. The dashes make little sense in the context of the sentence.

66. D: No punctuation is necessary within this phrase, because the conjunction joins two items in a series instead of two independent clauses. The comma within the conjunction is unnecessary, because there are two items in the series instead of three. The hyphen is unnecessary, because the conjunction joins two individual nouns instead of a two nouns that function as a single adjective.

67. C: The transitional expression "Additionally" makes the most sense in the context of the sentence, because it expresses the accumulation of concerns that led the Separatists to look for a haven outside of the Netherlands. Both "On the other hand" and "At the same time" suggest a contrast that is not called for in the context of the sentence. The expression "Consequently" suggests a cause-and-effect relationship that does not exist between the two sentences.

68. A: The sentence is correct as it is punctuated, because a comma is appropriate before a coordinating conjunction (as in question 62). All other forms of punctuation fail to recognize the relationship between the two clauses. The colon suggests a definition, expansion, or clarification that does not exist between the sentences. The comma without a conjunction is a comma splice that creates a run-on sentence.

69. A: The dash is appropriate in this case, because it creates a slightly dramatic pause between the two statements and offsets the desire of the Separatists to avoid too close a proximity to the influences of New World colonies that belonged to England. The comma would not be necessary in this case, because the conjunction "but" does not join two independent clauses. The lack of any punctuation makes the ideas run together awkwardly and does not give the reader enough indication of the meaning within the sentence. The semicolon creates a fragment.

70. D: The hyphen joins the two words and functions as a single adjective that modifies the noun "Massachusetts." The other usages of the hyphen and the lack of the hyphen cannot be correct in signaling the relationship among the three words.

Thank You

We at Mometrix would like to extend our heartfelt thanks to you, our friend and patron, for allowing us to play a part in your journey. It is a privilege to serve people from all walks of life who are unified in their commitment to building the best future they can for themselves.

The preparation you devote to these important testing milestones may be the most valuable educational opportunity you have for making a real difference in your life. We encourage you to put your heart into it—that feeling of succeeding, overcoming, and yes, conquering will be well worth the hours you've invested.

We want to hear your story, your struggles and your successes, and if you see any opportunities for us to improve our materials so we can help others even more effectively in the future, please share that with us as well. **The team at Mometrix would be absolutely thrilled to hear from you!** So please, send us an email (support@mometrix.com) and let's stay in touch.

If you feel as though you need additional help, please check out the other resources we offer:

Study Guide: http://MometrixStudyGuides.com/FSOT

Flashcards: http://MometrixFlashcards.com/FSOT